THE FLAMBOYANT MR. COLT
AND HIS DEADLY SIX-SHOOTER

The Flamboyant
MR. COLT
and His Deadly
SIX-SHOOTER

~ BERN KEATING ~

Doubleday & Company, Inc.
Garden City, New York
1978

ISBN: 0-385-12371-X
Library of Congress Catalog Card Number 78-8214

From *Punch:*

Oh, Colonel Colt, a thunderbolt
I'd buy for no small trifle;
But that can't be, and so let me
Get your revolving rifle.

I

January 22, 1814. To avenge the massacre of whites and blacks
at Fort Mims, in Alabama, sharpshooting militiamen from Tennessee, armed with the world-famed Kentucky flintlock rifle,
attacked braves of the Indian confederacy at Emuckfaw. The
Tennesseans were the same soldiers who would slaughter the
cream of the British Army a year later at New Orleans. At
Emuckfaw, Tennessee reeled back in bloody defeat.

January 24, 1814. Again, at Enotachopco Creek, the Indians
hurled back the militia and their single-shot flintlock rifles.

January 27, 1814. Led by Andrew Jackson, the stubborn militia, three thousand strong, attacked at Horseshoe Bend and
finally crushed the Indian confederacy of Creeks and Cherokees,
but only after frightful slaughter.

And those were woodland, farmer Indians, long since too
civilized to consider warfare the only honorable profession for a

male, as did the fierce tribes across the Mississippi. The vast central and western plains lay fallow, guarded by nomadic tribes. Those superb horsemen, armed with lance and bow, drifted across the land, denying it to sedentary white farmers and drovers who coveted those fertile seas of grass.

Not that Plains Indians were any more warlike than white men—far from it. The almost incredible fact was that the savages had better weapons and tactics for their terrain than technologically advanced whites, though whites were already half a century into the Industrial Revolution.

For two centuries, gunsmiths had slept over their art. They had turned out exquisitely beautiful instruments; many of their flintlock rifles were extraordinarily accurate within limited range. But their few small improvements in the flintlock arms were about as revolutionary as though Watt had invented an improved harness for horses instead of a steam engine, Whitney had developed a finer hand comb for cotton instead of a gin, Fulton had carved a more efficient canoe paddle instead of building a steamboat. The rifle had been a small advance over the smoothbore musket in range and accuracy, but in rate of fire the rifle was almost a step backward.

A skillful muzzle-loading rifleman today can recharge his weapon in about twenty seconds. And that is at the target range, where the only distraction is the good-natured ribbing of fellow competitors. Unless he was named John Wayne, a white settler facing the charge of a horde of whooping savages was bound to suffer hand tremors and a failure of concentration serious enough to affect his reloading technique. (On the field after the battle of Gettysburg, inspectors found unfired muzzleloaders crammed with five balls pounded one atop the other.)

Typically, a band of whites attacked in Indian lands fired a volley to inflict maximum casualties at the longest practicable range, then began frantically spilling powder and pumping ramrod to prepare a second shot. During the next, painful twenty seconds, a running warrior could cross 150 yards, or just about the maximum combat range of a musket. A mounted warrior, of course, could close from three times the effective combat range of single-shot muzzle-loaders.

In either case, afoot or mounted, the Indian warrior advanced under a cloud of arrows fired so fast that he could put six to ten in the air while the rifleman was ramming a single lead ball home and priming the pan. After his opening volley, if the white settler was not already bristling with arrows, he was likely to finish the fight using his firearm as a club in hand-to-hand combat.

Benjamin Franklin, who made an eternal reputation as a great sage just by not closing his eyes to the obvious, had recommended that the American military consider adopting the bow and arrow as the basic hand weapon because of its lethal rate of fire.

In 1814, the same year the Creeks threw back two assaults by Tennessee's riflemen, Joshua Shaw, of Philadelphia, produced the first percussion cap, a neat and compact package that would replace the clumsy and unreliable flintlock. But weapons still required reloading between shots, a pause that often proved fatal.

Also in 1814, on July 19, at a farm near Hartford, Connecticut, Sarah Caldwell Colt bore a third son to Christopher. They named him Samuel. He was destined to take the first great leap forward in hand weaponry in two centuries. His invention would make possible a multiplication of firepower that would revolutionize warfare worldwide and—of more immediate interest to the young United States—drive the Mexicans from Texas and the Indians from the western plains.

II

Sam's mother, Sarah, was the pampered daughter of Major John Caldwell, prominent soldier and wealthy merchant of Hartford. She doted on her children: Margaret (1806), Sarah Ann (1808), John (1810), Christopher, Jr. (1812), Sam (1814), and James (1816).

The major had at first opposed Sarah's courtship by Christopher Colt, a twenty-five-year-old speculator about to be run out of town, in the unkind custom of the day, merely for being broke after a series of unlucky ventures. Bowing to the inevitable, the major had permitted the marriage and had installed Christopher in the infamous Triangle Trade: the shipping of slaves from Africa to the West Indies and their sale there for sugar, the conversion in New England of the West Indies sugar to rum, and its export to Africa to pay for more slaves. Puritanical Yankees made fortunes trading in human flesh and booze;

Christopher joined in heartily and became satisfactorily rich. During the War of 1812, however, British privateers ruined him by waylaying his cargoes on the high seas. The financial panic of 1819 finished him off in Hartford. By 1820 the major and his son-in-law were bankrupt. The major retired; Christopher moved to Ware, Massachusetts, where he set up a silk mill. A silkworm boom had collapsed in France because of the prohibitive cost of unwinding cocoons by hand. Christopher Colt harnessed a millrace from Ware Pond to process the cocoons by machine—a move that foreshadowed his third son's industrial genius.

According to legend, about the time of the move to Massachusetts, the six-year-old Samuel found a discarded horse pistol, dismantled it, and rebuilt it with parts he cannibalized from broken pistols in a gunsmith's junk box. Probably an apocryphal story, but maybe not. Sam soon displayed a well-documented precocity in mechanical matters and a ravenous curiosity about tools and machines.

Shortly after the move, on June 16, 1821, the gentle and indulgent Sarah died of tuberculosis, a month before Sam's seventh birthday. On March 12, 1823, Christopher married Olivia Sargent, the daughter of a mechanic-engineer of Hartford. The family found that Olivia was no substitute for their dead mother, for she almost instantly cleaned out the house, scattering children about the countryside with small regard for their comfort or happiness. She farmed out Sarah Ann, for instance, to relatives who put her to grinding menial labor.

Sam was luckier. He lived with a farmer in Glastonbury, Connecticut, and apparently was reasonably well treated. The moral climate of the time and place did not suit the restless youngster, however, because there is evidence he was disciplined for disturbing the Sabbath by firing a horse pistol, possibly the one he had rebuilt.

The legacy of the sour religious zealots who had founded New England was still strong. Blue laws forbade running on the Sabbath or even walking in the garden—or anywhere else, for that matter, except "reverently to and from church." The disciples of the Christ who had preached universal love forbade kissing of husband and wife on the Sabbath—even prescribed that "no mother shall kiss her child upon the Sabbath-day."

Little wonder that Sam's shattering of the Sabbath quiet with a large-caliber pistol offended Connecticut's sensibilities and provoked punishment.

Though Sam was a miserable student of the classical curriculum, he discovered in the farmer's library the encyclopedic Compendium of Knowledge and was entranced. Reading that volume, which supposedly summarized all of man's knowledge, inflamed his mind with imaginative applications of science to solving man's practical problems.

Given the oppressive moral atmosphere in Connecticut that did not permit a high-spirited lad to tinker with explosives on a Sunday, and given also Sam's quickening interest in machinery, it is no surprise that he grabbed at his father's invitation to return to Ware and help in the factory only twelve months after his arrival.

For three years, Sam toiled amid the din of clattering machines, their parts meshing, pumping, clacking, whirling in a mechanical ballet that suited the young mechanic's temperament. He witnessed not only the introduction of machinery into a trade that had always been practiced by housewives on a hearthside spinning wheel and loom, he also witnessed the beginnings of division of labor, with each laborer concentrating on a single task.

Among the silk-mill specialists was a William T. Smith, who ran the chemical laboratory. Apparently Smith and young Colt tinkered with gunpowder recipes. They also fooled around with nitrous oxide, the "laughing gas" that gives those who whiff it a euphoric high. It is still one of the most valuable anesthetics in modern surgical practice, but Smith and young Colt seemed more interested in its mind-bending qualities. (Smith would probably be run off the place today for contributing to the delinquency of a minor.)

Sometime during 1828 or 1829, when Sam was about fourteen, he enrolled at Amherst Academy, a new school but already famed for its faculty. The high-powered teachers apparently did not impress Sam, however, for he was often disciplined.

Sam got into serious trouble, again over firearms. School regulations prohibited discharging firearms "either in shooting at game or at mark, or for amusement in any manner." Sam was caught firing his trusty horse pistol and fled to Ware rather than sit through a session with the formidable Reverend Royal Ashburn, president of the school's board.

Undaunted by his unhappy experiences with gunpowder, he was soon passing about a handbill reading:

Sam'l Colt Will Blow a Raft Sky-High on
Ware Pond, July 4, 1829

As Colt told Congress years later:

The idea of Submarine explosions for the purpose of Harbour defence was conceived by me as early as the year 1829 while studying in the laboratory of a bleeching and colouring establishment at Ware Vilage Massachusetts, and I made sundry experiments on a small scale at that time. . . .

A young mechanic named Elisha Root recalled the Ware Pond experiment:

> It had been noised around that a youngster—one Sam Colt—would blow up a raft on the pond that day, and so I with other apprentices of the neighborhood walked some way to see the sight. An explosion was produced, but the raft was by no means blown sky-high.

In fact, the explosion pretty well missed the raft and lifted instead a geyser of filthy mud and water that cascaded down on the assembled spectators in their holiday costume. Outraged by what they thought was a deliberate prank rather than a failed experiment, the crowd threatened Sam with a thrashing, but Elisha Root rescued him.

After the crowd dispersed to sop off the mud and change clothes, Root asked Colt how he had passed the electric current through the water to detonate the mine.

"Simple. I wrapped the wire in tarred cloth."

Consider that at that date famed inventors, including the great Robert Fulton, father of the paddle-wheel steamboat, had struggled to construct a practicable underwater mine without notable success; yet a fifteen-year-old school dropout had put together an eminently successful submarine infernal machine and had, unaided, solved the vexatious problem of passing an electric current from shore to his torpedo so that he could set it off at will.

Young Colt had already written a Mr. Samuel Lawrence, of Boston, asking him to use his influence as a merchant to find Sam a berth as midshipman in training to become a navigator and ship's officer. Owners of the brig *Corvo* agreed to take him aboard. On August 2, 1830, Mr. Lawrence sent Sam's father a bill for ninety dollars to pay for a quadrant and nautical almanac, sea clothing, and other tools of the sailor's trade—including, most importantly as it turned out, a $1.00 jackknife. He added:

The ship sailed this morning. The last time I saw Sam he was in tarpaulin, checked shirt, checked trousers, on the fore topsail yard, loosing the topsail. This was famous at a first going-off. He is a manly fellow, and I have no doubt will do credit to all concerned. He was in good spirits on departure. . . .

The brig was carrying cotton fabrics and a load of missionaries. By September 11, 1830, Sam had crossed the equator and thus become a true sea rover. A month later he rounded the Cape of Good Hope, into the Indian Ocean. On December 17, 1830, the brig made a landfall at the mouth of the Hooghly River, in India, after a voyage of more than seventeen thousand miles. Sam wandered the exotic streets of Calcutta while the brig took on new cargo. The ship returned by way of London. Somewhere during that year's voyage, in London or Calcutta, Sam may have seen a model of the flintlock with rotating chambered breech designed by Elisha Collier, of Boston, in 1813, patented in England, and built there in some numbers for use by British troops in India. Sam later denied it.

It is certain that during the trip, with his $1.00 jackknife, he whittled from a discarded block the model of a pistol with rotating six-chambered cylinder. Far more important than the revolving cylinder, which was by no means a new idea, as witness the Collier flintlock, was his use of pawl and ratchet—the same gear that locked a capstan in position and prevented the running away of a cable under tension when sailors released pressure on the capstan bars. Sam may have picked up the idea from watching ten thousand turns of the capstan aboard the

Corvo, or it may have sprung spontaneously from his inventive mind. In either case, the use of a pawl to rotate the cylinder as the hammer was cocked, automatically presenting a fresh load for the next shot, is what made his design revolutionary.

Back in Ware, though his father and stepmother urged him to sign on for another cruise and make the sea his lifetime work, Sam persuaded his father to pay for construction of a working model of the wooden revolver. They hired a gunsmith named Anson Chase for a down payment of fifteen dollars, and he began work on a pistol and also on a rifle with similar chambered cylinder.

Sam's father apparently became impatient, for he wrote to Captain Abner Bassett, of Norwich, Connecticut, about a berth for Sam. The whaler answered, on January 10, 1832, that plans were afoot for a whaling voyage of twenty-six to thirty months. He invited Sam to join the ship's company.

But Sam was having no more of the sea. He had returned to the Ware chemical laboratory, where he assembled a portable rig for making nitrous oxide. Advertising himself as the "Celebrated Dr. Coult of New York, London, and Calcutta," he tried a few lectures on chemistry in neighboring towns. (Why he chose to misspell his name is a mystery, though in general his spelling was so wretched that there is no reason even his own name should have escaped mutilation.) His scientific lecture may have gone over passably well or not, but his demonstrations of the effects of laughing gas on volunteers from the audience brought down the house.

Encouraged by the take on his experimental tour, Sam wrote his father that he was not going back to sea but embarking on a new (and purposely vague) enterprise. His father wrote him one of those homiletic letters full of advice on manners, morals, and application to duty that fathers of those innocent times fondly believed were solemnly heeded by young sons.

Sam picked up the Chase rifle and pistol and left for Washington with another letter from his father, which probably carried much more weight for the young man. It was a letter of introduction to Henry Ellsworth, a friend of Christopher Colt and, happily for the young inventor, the U.S. commissioner of patents.

Mr. Ellsworth wrote to Christopher on February 20, 1832:

> Samuel is now here getting along very well with his new invention. Scientific men and the great folks speak highly of the thing.—I hope he will be well rewarded for his labors. I shall be happy to aid him. He obtained 300 here at the bank with my endorsement. . . .

Mr. Ellsworth recommended that Sam not apply for a patent on the basis of his crude models but, rather, deposit them in the secret lockup of the Patent Office and take out a caveat—a provisional kind of affidavit to establish priority against the time when Sam had adequately improved his invention.

To raise money for more gunsmith fees, Sam hit the road again with his laughing-gas show. Pushing his equipment in a handcart, Sam worked his way northward, giving shows in small towns and crossroads settlements along the way. From New York City, he took the steamboat to Providence. Years later, a legend grew up that cholera broke out on the ship and he was called on to treat the patients because of his self-proclaimed status as a scientist and the honorific "Dr." on his handbills. His treatments worked as well as those of a proper medical doctor, the story goes, and that part could well have been true, given the level of medicine at the time. Colt certainly had the gall to impersonate a medical doctor, but the story is almost certainly apocryphal.

His shows were enormously popular. An advertising broadside published in Portland, Maine, on October 13, 1832, informs the public that his nitrous oxide

. . . when inhaled into the lungs produced the most astonishing effects upon the nervous system; that some individuals were disposed to laugh, sing, and dance; others, to recitation and declamation, and that the great number had an irresistible propensity to muscular exertion, such as wrestling, boxing, and with innumerable fantastic feats. In short, the sensations produced by it are highly pleasurable, and are not followed by debility.

Sam assured his public that his audiences were composed

. . . of Ladies and Gentlemen of the first respectability— and many Ladies have inhaled the GAS at select Exhibitions. Those Ladies who may be anxious of witnessing the Exhibition . . . may be assured that . . . not a shadow of impropriety attends the Exhibition, to shock the most modest. . . .

He also offered to sell private whiffs at fifty cents a dose during morning hours. Considering that the finest New York restaurants of the time served a full dinner for fifteen cents or less, the price of a laughing-gas high was not low.

As the money rolled in, Sam was paying it out to gunsmiths— to True & Davis, of Albany, New York, for instance, who made a set of forgings, and eleven dollars to Samuel Gibson to assemble them into a pistol. (That historic weapon early disappeared.)

On December 21, 1833, he wrote Anson Chase a demand

note promising to pay twenty-six dollars for a pistol, apparently the same first pistol that, legends hold, blew up on the first shot. Actually, it suffered only a small accident that showed up a minor error in design. Sam continued to urge Chase on and by year's end had paid him $123.85.

Sam hit the road again. In Baltimore he teamed with a Joseph E. Walker, who ran a museum of sorts and gave regular shows in the museum's lecture hall. By March of 1834 he had engaged a gunsmith, A. T. Baxter, who had in turn assigned one John Pearson to work on Colt's rifle. During the next seven weeks, Sam paid Pearson more than four hundred dollars for materials and work on two rifles and several pistols. In another month Pearson left Baxter to work solely for Colt.

His contract, dated June 22, 1834, reads:

> I John Pearson agree to work for Mr. Samuel Colt Twelve Months at Ten Dollars per week, Ten hours in each day (Sundays excepted) out of which Wagies to Pay Shop and Forge Rent to John Coalt Four Dollars per month—I to draw my wagies weekley. In case disagreement eather party have the prevelage of closing the contract by giving One Months notice.

Leaving Pearson to work on his invention, Sam made a swing through South Carolina and Georgia and northward to New York by boat. He checked in briefly at Baltimore and then went to Montreal, where he performed the extraordinary feat of memorizing his lecture in French almost overnight, an achievement that argues a higher level of verbal skill than the written English he has left behind would indicate. (Not only was Colt's spelling eccentric, he was left-handed and wrote a difficult scrawl.)

To keep Pearson at the grindstone, Colt sent money regularly by way of the museum keeper, Walker. Sam's Baltimore connection was also dabbling in inventions, for he was financing production of an "ariel ship" that was a hybrid balloon-kite with some kind of propeller drive. Walker wrote Colt inquiring about a Canadian patent, and Sam reported it would cost one hundred dollars. Far from sending it along, however, Walker had to duck out in the night when the aircraft failed to fly and friends who had put up money on Walker's recommendation wanted their investment back. He reopened his museum in Richmond, Virginia.

A cholera epidemic drove Sam from Montreal and later from Quebec City. He prospered in Saint John, New Brunswick, and bought a few bolts of cloth as an investment, for he planned to smuggle them into the States for a fat profit—an enterprise by no means frowned on by the free traders of New England in that day. He was caught at customs and forfeited most of the cloth.

Other reverses forced him to write conciliatory letters to Pearson promising early payment of back wages and urging him not only to continue the work but to pay for more supplies from his own pocket.

On Walker's invitation, Sam traveled to Richmond to put on his shows for 50 per cent of the gate.

To hang on to Pearson, Colt wrote him on January 17, 1835:

> I improve this lieshour moment in informing you that my affairs here are like to terminate as wel as I had expected & on Monday or Tuesday next I wil make you a remitance that wil inable you to commence my work. You can therefore make your arrangements accordingly At al events dont ingage yourself to aneyone until you hear from

me again which wil be on Monday or Tuesday next (Possatively).

Two days later he did send money, but he added an order for Pearson to buy accessories and tools. He also sent instructions for ornamentation of an experimental shotgun.

Take it to the ingraver underneath the Museum or to some other good ingraver & have him ingrave the Colts heads in the center of which I want my name "S COLT P R" ingraved. . . .

That is first word of the design that characterized early Colt weapons—four horse heads within a rectangle.

Colt told Pearson he intended to hire assistants, but he also made a new wage proposal that was an unexplained cut in salary, only nine dollars weekly for sixty hours or ten dollars for seventy-two hours. Pearson wrote an angry reply:

. . . your offer of $10 for twelve hours each day I take as an insult for you to offer me.

He raged on with sarcasms about having to buy candles to work late into the night

. . . and then wait 6 months or your pleasure for my pay as I have done . . . the money you sent me wont pay all your bills and you order me to buy a Barrel and flask and pay for a forging and all these things which will take a great part of it. I think it nothing but just and right that you pay me my money. . . . For I am neither willing nor able to hazard my Time or Money on your work anymore. So you can use your own pleasure whether you employ me or not. . . .

Colt dug up seventy-five dollars and sent it with a note saying:

> Dont be allarmed about your wages, nothing shal be rong on my part, but doo wel for me & you shal fare wel.

Pearson went back to work and shipped the engraved shotgun and supplies for making laughing gas to Colt at Richmond. He also sent a progress report:

> I am getting on with the work as well as I can but it has been such cold weather and this shop so cold that I had like to be frose. But I hope it will be milder soon. I have got our pistol to work very well and am getting it ready for stocking . . . but I am out of money and the rent is due today and I want some more wood for fire. . . .

With his gas generator replenished, Sam took to the road again on a loop around Virginia. By March 25, 1835, he was able to send Pearson fifty dollars.

On April 11, 1835, Sam moved into a room in Baltimore. Pearson had several weapons in various stages of progress, all of them promising to be well enough designed and machined for patent models. Sam hired an assistant, and the three men moved into larger quarters to rush the work to completion.

Carrying a model rifle and pistol, on June 17, 1835, Sam called on his cousin Dudley Selden, a wealthy lawyer in New York. Dudley apparently considered the models patentable and advised Sam to draw up his application pictures.

Sam was coasting so close to bankruptcy he had to pawn one of his pistols to pay for the ride to Washington with his model rifle and pistol. He engaged a draftsman to draw his plates for sixteen dollars.

Confident of the American patent, Sam felt that he needed

protection in France and England also, for in those days they were the two most technologically advanced countries in the world and could pirate his designs at no profit to him. Sam's father lent him one thousand dollars and took as security a one-eighth interest in the hypothetical patent. Dudley's father, Joseph Selden, lent another one thousand dollars on a similar guarantee.

Flush for a change, Sam deposited $150 to Pearson's account in a Baltimore bank and raised him to twelve dollars a week. He picked up a shotgun and pistol and sailed from New York in late August 1835. He arrived in Liverpool on September 13, 1835. A few days later, he hired the patent attorney John Hawkins, and the legal machine began to grind. In a startlingly short time Sam received from the High Chancery Court notice that King William IV

. . . by His Letters Patent under the Great Seal of Great Britain . . . the twenty second day of October . . . did give and grant unto me, the said Samuel Colt, His especial license, full power and sole privelege and authority, that I . . . from time to time and at all times during the term of years therein expressed, should and lawfully might make, use, exceicise and vond, within England, Wales, and the Town of Berwick upon Tweed, my Invention of Certain improvements applicable to firearms. . . .

Sam had the model pistol polished, blued, and engraved with scrollwork, and on October 30, 1835, he deposited it to complete the patent process, for a total cost of over six hundred dollars.

Scotland had a flourishing firearms industry and a separate patent system, so Sam headed north.

Somehow in Scotland he met a beautiful young girl—perhaps

no more than sixteen years old—called Caroline Henshaw, apparently a German national with almost no English, despite her name. She also probably could not read or write. She had come to Scotland and been stranded by God knows what circumstances. Samuel was so touched he married her. She traveled with him to France, where he engaged a M. Perpigna as patent attorney.

The soundness of his designs and the practicality of his invention are attested by the fact that M. Perpigna—a solid French bourgeois—actually lent his unknown American client half the cost of the application, an act that staggers the mind of anybody who has had dealings with the French bourgeoisie.

On December 3, 1835, the young couple boarded the *Albany* at Le Havre for a thirty-four-day crossing to the United States.

The American patent came through on February 25, 1836. (By a fateful coincidence, the Mexican dictator Santa Anna had just besieged the Alamo.) The American patent date's coming three months after the French award was potentially dangerous, for by a quirk of French law his French patent was good only till he received a later patent in another country. The American award threw his invention open to quite legal copying in France. And yet, curiously, French arms makers never took advantage of the loophole, for only a very few unauthorized copies ever appeared in that country.

The patent depended on three innovations: 1. rotation of a many-chambered cylinder breech in a single-barreled firearm actuated by cocking the hammer; 2. locking and unlocking of the cylinder by the cocking action; and 3. placing partitions between the nipples to prevent side flare from the fired cap igniting them all.

It was time to start making instead of spending money on Colt's invention.

III

With his patents secure, Sam was no longer bound to secrecy. Indeed, the more publicity the better, and no American merchant ever realized more keenly the value of advertising and a little grease for the appropriate palms.

In the spring of 1836, shortly after receiving his patent, he carried models to Washington and managed a demonstration for President Andrew Jackson.

Throughout history, young soldiers have been sent to war armed with weapons obsolete by a generation but still issued by senior brass because they were the latest weapons when the aging generals were young lions on the battlefield.

Andrew Jackson was no more farsighted than other senescent warriors. He should have had a keen sense of the unreliability of the old-time arms, for an assassin had attacked him only a few weeks earlier and had failed because both his pistols had misfired. But the crusty old man, far from being impressed by a repeating firearm, ordered for the Army a new issue of .54-caliber flintlock pistols—flintlocks, twenty-two years after the invention of the percussion cap.

Undaunted by the President's rebuff, Colt threw parties for anybody in Washington he considered important and sent the bills to Selden. Throughout his life, Sam lived high, ran up prodigious expenses, drank heartily, and cynically counted as much on the venality of government officers as on the value of his invention for furthering his cause. He was a strapping big fellow, at least six feet tall, with a quick and powerful left hand in his frequent brawls. If we can judge by the superb portrait painted by his friend Samuel Morse, an eminent artist before he became better known as the inventor of the telegraph, Colt was a handsome fellow and an imposing figure of a man. During those convivial sessions in Washington, however, when he drank cup for cup with the nation's most powerful politicians, he probably was planting in himself the seeds of two maladies that broke his powerful frame at what should have been the prime of his life. Sam's mature years were racked with the agonies of gout and rheumatic fever, neither illness one that responds well to alcoholic treatment.

The conservative attorney Selden, an incredibly long-suffering man, protested Colt's extravagance:

> You use money as if it were drawn from an inexhaustible mine. I have no belief in undertaking to raise the character of your gun by old Madeira. . . .

He impressed some journalists, however, for on February 24, 1836, F. S. Blair, of the Washington *Post,* wrote:

> I have tried the newly improved pistol of Mr. Colt and

found that it shot exceedingly well— In my opinion it will proove a very great improvement in firearms.

On March 2, 1836, there appeared the following dispatch simultaneously in the Baltimore *Republic,* the Charleston *Courier,* and the Washington *Globe:*

> We have seen samples of the invention which is certainly exceedingly ingenious and meritorious. Its advantages are great. You have in a small pocket pistol always six charges which may be discharged in succession as fast as you can snap the lock, and when exhausted a new cartridge box may be applied in the twinkling of an eye by which means a continued stream of fire may be constantly kept up.

Just three days later, on March 5, 1836, Dudley Selden supervised passage of a bill through the New Jersey legislature incorporating the Patent Arms Manufacturing Company of New Jersey, its purpose given as the making of "arms, machinery and cutlery." Possibly because there were many Colts in Paterson, the corporate officers decided to build their factory on the Passaic River near that town.

Sam wrote a letter on March 9, 1836, assigning the patent to the company in exchange for royalties; temporary officers set out to sell stock.

By August 1836, thirty-three stockholders had subscribed much of the three hundred thousand dollars permitted by charter. Dudley Selden, with 240 shares, was in deepest. Sam had one hundred shares and his father fifty. Most of the money was only pledged against a small down payment.

Meanwhile, back in Baltimore, the same old story. Long-suffering Pearson was still grinding away at improving Colt's designs and writing angry letters demanding money, with little success. Sam stalled with a promise that Pearson would be paid after the company advanced Sam one thousand dollars, on April 18, 1834.

On April 23, 1834, Pearson wrote:

> . . . I can place no confidence in what you write me as you said you was to receive $1000 on the 18th inst after which you should come on here immediately but here it is satirday and you are not come yet nor very likely not one foot nearer than when you last wrote. . . . If you was disapointed in getting the money you might have borrowed as much as would satisfy me as you say you have got through all the difficulty.

And indeed Sam was borrowing heavily from Dudley and his own father—between January 10 and June 9, 1836, more than $2,000—yet he sent only a pittance to his faithful gunsmith.

Pearson wrote on May 9, 1836:

> . . . I suppose you thought you had done fine to send me $100 . . . but your account is now over $100 more. . . . I shall expect some money next week or I wil stop work for I can get Half a Dozen places of work and get my Pay every week. You are in a Devil of a hurry but not to pay your men.

And with that last, pitiful plaint the shabbily treated Baltimore artisan disappears from history.

In his place came Pliny Lawton, from Springfield, Massachusetts, site of the United States Armory, though there is no evidence Lawton ever worked there. He somehow came to the notice of Christopher Colt as a skilled artisan and accepted an invitation to organize the Paterson factory. He arrived May 16,

1836, and discovered quickly that the handmade models of Pearson had many bugs for machine manufacture. Colt turned the problems of production over to Lawton and took his selling talents to Washington, hoping the military would prefer his weapons over archaic arms from earlier wars or the increasingly ingenious designs of competitors.

During one of Sam's periodic visits back to the Paterson factory, Dudley Selden witnessed the accidental bursting of a gun. In fright and anger he told Colt his contract with the company was ended. Colt lashed back by writing on March 3, 1837, to Lawton:

> This is to inform you that my interest with the Patent Arms Man'y Co has entially seases the reason for which you are no doubt better informed than myself I therefore strictly forbid you as the acting agent of said Company from proseeding any ferther in the manufacturing of rotary repeting guns that contain any one or the whole of my clames.

(Dudley Selden had once written Sam, "I wish that you would so write English that I could show the letters. . . . Buy a dictionary." Which admonition Sam obviously never heeded.)

The quarrel blew over, Sam and Pliny again attacked design problems that caused multiple shooting on a single trigger pull. They experimented with beveling the chamber fronts but eventually settled on a loading lever strong enough to ram home an oversize ball that sealed the chamber.

Pressure from several designers forced the Ordnance Department to announce a competition, for June 16, 1837, at West Point.

Besides Colt's designs, the Army tested the Cochran rifle, a monstrosity mounting a flat circular magazine with charges radiating from a center pivot so that one charge was always pointed menacingly into the rifleman's eyeball, an unnerving sight in the days when firing a repeating weapon frequently touched off all charges at once. Another weapon tested was a breech-loading single-shot firing a paper cartridge, designed by an Irish nobleman, Baron Hackett. Also on trial was a revolving-cylinder weapon designed by Daniel Leavitt and patented only seven weeks before, on April 29, 1837. As controls, the Army fired the standard service weapons of the day.

Colt had allowed the Ordnance Board to force him to enter an unwieldy monster of a repeating musket, because Army specifications called for musket calibers of almost three quarters of an inch. Events proved he should have rejected the specifications as unsuitable to repeating weapons and unnecessary for modern warfare. During test volleys, his gross weapon suffered several accidental double shots.

The ordnance report said the supervising officers were satisfied with weapons already in service. The Cochran gun with the wheel magazine they found downright dangerous—to the user, that is.

Colt's weapon, the report said,

. . . may be usefully applied in special cases—such as in stationary defense, entrenchments, blockhouses, perhaps, too, in the naval service, in the tops of ships, to cover or repel boarders, and in boat service.—Notwithstanding these objects favorable to it, the board is unanimous in opinion, that from the complicated construction of this arm, its liability to accidents (one having occurred on the 21st of June) in firing, and for other reasons before noticed, that it is not adapted to the general purposes of the service.

Again the press was more impressed than the military, for a

New York reporter repeated the old chestnut about a recruit who put nineteen balls into his musket to avoid the necessity of reloading in battle; the paper said the West Point trial of Colt's arms had demonstrated that the recruit's device had become practicable.

The New York *Courier and Enquirer* report from West Point, published June 29, 1837, was more emphatic, even scornful of military stuffiness:

> The by-standers seemed to consider Colt's the favorite. He fired 18 charges in the incredible short space of 58 seconds—and the accuracy and penetration of the ball proved as good as the ordinary rifle; indeed the penetration is said to be better. . . . I have no doubt Colt's . . . must meet with the approbation of the public and get into general use with sportsmen, whatever may be the views of the army in relation to its adoption in the service. . . . For an Indian campaign it must be invaluable. One shot would bring the Indian from his seclusion, and the remaining nine in the cylinder which would be discharged in one minute would made sad havock.

Nevertheless, the West Point trial was a failure, so far as sales were concerned.

After that failure, the short-tempered Selden again fired Colt and again took him back after a cooling-off period.

Lawton was grinding away in the factory, turning out eight-shot repeating rifles, one model with a short barrel—about twenty-four inches—and an identical rifle with a barrel from twenty-nine to thirty-two inches. Calibers varied from rifle to rifle but were about .45. Because of the variation in bore width, bullet molds and other accessories were custom made for each piece and marked with the same serial number.

Colt proposed to sell the rifles in New York or Washington at
$100 wholesale and $125 retail; in New Orleans, the supply
base for Texas, he foresaw an even better sale, at $125 whole-
sale and $150 retail.

Dudley Selden and Colt carried on a querulous correspondence, Selden complaining that Colt spent too much and
returned little, Colt arguing that the company was laggard in
offering production models for sale.

Finally, on December 18, 1837, the first advertisement appeared in the New York *Courier and Enquirer* and the *Evening
Star* notifying the public that Colt's repeating rifles "are now for
the first time offered for sale . . . and in beauty and workmanship are fully equal to the highest finished Rifles imported from
England." The advertisement also noted the rifles were "con-
structed for eight charges" and had won the gold medal of the
American Institute at its exhibition of advances in firearms design.

In making that gold-medal announcement, incidentally, the
Institute issued an extraordinarily myopic statement:

> Some have expressed apprehension that the perfection
> of firearms may lead to extended destruction of human
> life. The analogy derived from gunpowder affords a com-
> plete answer. All the great inventions of the world have
> tended to humanize and civilize. The genius of the arts is
> averse to bloodshed, and wars will diminish in proportion
> as the arts progress and engross the attention and exertions
> of mankind.

The Stone Age inventor of the war club almost certainly
defended it with the argument that it was a weapon of such hor-
ribly destructive potential that it made war forevermore un-
thinkable.

At Castle Garden, an open-air amusement park at the Battery, at the southern tip of Manhattan, a demonstration of rapid fire by Colt rifles entertained a large crowd, but few of the delighted spectators were rich enough to pay $125 for a repeating rifle. Colt realized that the big money was in mass production, and the only client big enough to afford wholesale lots was the military.

IV

Mixed with the fossilized brains that survive to high rank in the military are sometimes a few lively brains that somehow also work their way up, despite the Old Boy Mutual Protective Society. One such, in 1838, was Lieutenant Colonel W. S. Harney, commanding the 2d Dragoons. The Army of that day had no real cavalry, incidentally, because the massed bayonets of infantry blocks had thwarted the traditional cavalry charge. Dragoons used horses for fast transport but dismounted to fight as infantry. Nevertheless, in the absence of real cavalry, dragoons enjoyed the traditional elite status of mounted troops.

Since 1835 the Seminole Indians, of Florida, had been at war with the United States. Regular troops had been frustrated by that deadly gap of firepower between volleys of single-shot weapons. The Indians had early developed a tactic of feinting with a weak attack to bring on a volley and then pressing home, through the dense undergrowth of semitropical Florida, an attack at close quarters.

The Seminole trouble began when the U. S. Army ordered the Florida Indians to sell their cattle, on December 1, 1835, to free themselves of encumbrance for their forced emigration to the other side of the Mississippi River. Many Indians complied. Unknown bushwhackers ambushed one of the most influential chieftains, Charley Emathla, and killed him on his way home. They scattered his money on his body to show their contempt for the cattle sale. The public, the Army, and very probably the Indians themselves blamed a young firebrand named Osceola and his band of diehards who refused emigration to strange lands.

In succeeding months Indian bands ravaged sugar plantations (which never did reopen and today lie in picturesque ruins). On December 28, 1835, Indians shot the commanding general in Florida and a lieutenant within sight of Fort King and killed a party of sutlers trying to round up their trade goods and rush them into the fort.

When news came in that, on the same day, Indians had ambushed two companies of soldiers and killed all but three of 111, the Army realized the Indians were more than a nuisance.

To wipe out the Indian menace in a single stroke, the commanding general massed five hundred mounted militia and 250 regulars and marched on an Indian concentration reported at Withlacoochee.

On New Year's Eve, 1835, the regulars were thrown back while trying to cross the Withlacoochee River.

During the next year, the Army steadily beefed up its strength, with little effect. Indian raids struck here and there, keeping the frontier terrorized. Patrols could not come to grips with the marauders, who struck and slipped away into the wilderness.

Osceola came in to powwow late in 1837 and was captured while under a flag of truce. He died in captivity, but the fight went on.

On Christmas Day, 1837, a colonel named Zachary Taylor, with about eight hundred men, found four hundred Indians on an island in the swamp, lying behind prepared positions. Attackers had to cross a morass of mud and sawgrass. The Indians had cut a clear field of fire in front of their position. Colonel Taylor drove the Indians from the field (easy enough to do, since Indians virtually never fought for territory but only to inflict damage). In doing so, he lost twenty-six killed and 112 wounded. It was the first and last true pitched battle of the war.

The regulars were baffled by an enemy that struck where and when they wished and vanished before the slow rate of army firepower could inflict more than minimal damage.

Somewhere, probably at the West Point competition that Dudley Selden had dubbed a failure, Colonel William Harney had been impressed by the firepower of Colt's repeating rifles. By reading between the lines of existing correspondence, it appears that Colonel Harney promised to buy one hundred rifles for trial in Florida and Colt agreed to deliver them.

About the time of the Christmas Day battle, Colonel Harney wrote Colt from Fort Law, on the St. John's River, in eastern Florida:

> I have barely time to tell you that I have been greatly disappointed in not having received the guns yet. I mentioned what I had done to Genl. Jesup who approved of *everything*. If you have not started them yet lose no time in doing so for I wish them very much. I am still more

confident that they are the only things that will finish the *infernal war*. If you can bring one hundred Genl Jesup will take them all. Try also to bring some pistols.

Sam had been trying to talk the directors into consigning a lot of rifles to him for sale at ninety dollars each in South Carolina (then troubled by one of its recurrent threats to secede from the Union).

Remembering the blithe way Sam had once hocked the company's samples to pay for a trip farther south, the directors had refused to let him out of sight with any more pawnable materials. Colonel Harney's letter gave him a bit of muscle, however, and some assurance that he just might unload the arms legitimately before his road debts drove him back to the pawnshop. Nevertheless, the directors still insisted that a cousin and fellow shareholder, Roswell L. Colt, endorse Sam's note to cover the cost of one hundred rifles. Early in February 1838 Sam loaded them and himself aboard a steamer for Charleston, South Carolina.

He carried with him several pistols in different sizes, probably only models to be displayed to officers as sales samples. Knowing Sam's impulsiveness in sales technique, Lawton wrote him warning him that if the officers showed interest in the biggest "belt" model, he must on no account sell his sample, as it was apparently the only model extant on which Lawton could base further production.

Arrived at Camp Jupiter, near present-day Palm Beach, Colt was disappointed to sell only thirty of his one hundred rifles. Colonel Harney persuaded the general to increase the order to fifty. In combat, the delighted dragoons reported the weapons a tremendous success. As early as March 10, 1838, only a few days after issue of the repeating rifles, a board of officers of the

2d Dragoons issued a report with a foreword signed by Colonel Harney:

> I must beg leave to state here that I (a native Tennessean) have been all my life accustomed to the use of a Rifle, and after a full examination of Mr. Colt's gun, I feel pleasure in stating that I concur fully in opinion with the board; and I do assure you that sooner I would use any other Rifle myself, I would use none.

The board reported that from one hundred yards and again from two hundred yards the shot penetrated two inches into hard green pitch pine trees. Accuracy was high at all ranges.

Most impressive, however, was the report on celerity of fire: two receivers of eight charges each fired in thirty-one seconds; one receiver reloaded and fired in forty-eight seconds.

> . . . as regards celerity or rapidity of firing, it is as great as could be desired, and even greater than most occasions will require.

The board reported sinking the rifle under water for several minutes with no adverse effect.

Final recommendation was to arm one hundred specially picked dragoons as a shock troop for emergencies.

Sam received a draft of $6,250 for the rifles and twenty-five dollars for percussion caps. He probably also sold some of his sample pistols to a few officers. The draft was drawn on quartermaster headquarters at St. Augustine and Sam hurried there by sea to collect.

Blocked by a sandbar across the harbor mouth, on April 10, 1838, his vessel had to lay on and off while Colt and three others tried to go ashore in the ship's small boat. It capsized in the surf. The four clung to their craft for four hours till hauled ashore by local rescuers. The next day, Sam wrote the sad news to Dudley:

> I should send you the avails of my florida adventure by this mail but unluckily it is still in the serf on the Beach with most of our other luggage that was with us in the Boate. . . .

Sam held some hope that his trunk would wash ashore with the drafts intact, but he never saw them again.

Dudley Selden and some other officers of the company were angry and skeptical about Sam's report on how he had lost the money, though reflection would have convinced them that even with the most evil intentions there is virtually no way Sam could have converted a government draft to his own use without instant detection. His cousin Roswell Colt came to his defense again and temporarily covered his loss.

On June 21, 1838, a duplicate draft came through from Washington, representing by far the largest sale the company had made—and even more important, a sale to soldiers in combat, soldiers eager to endorse the product.

V

In the early fall of 1838, Sam and Lawton built up the stock of the largest-size pistol, called a "belt" model and catalogued as No. 5. This largest pistol of the line was a serious weapon, capable of great accuracy—extraordinary accuracy for a pistol—and it delivered a hard punch.

Calling on his cousin again to endorse his note, Colt drew a consignment of seventy-three assorted arms and accessories and headed for Washington. When he encountered the usual sluggishness of high rank to new ideas, he suggested that Jesse Hoyt, a Patent Arms Company stockholder and friend of the President and of the Secretary of the Navy, write letters to his two cronies to smooth Colt's way.

> . . . with a little "Legerdemain" . . . I think I may be able to obtain an order to make a brace of our belt pistols

for every officer in the Navey for I am confidant that the
officers would be glad to use arms of my construction to
protect their cowardly selves at the Government Expence
when they would not concent to put them in the hands of
Soldiers or Marines.

Sales lagged. Colonel George Bomford, head of the Ordnance Department and an officer with a distinguished past, had
reached that age and rank at which extreme rigidity sets in for
all but the most imaginative officers. He flatly opposed Colt's
innovations. Colt was not alone in suspecting that the colonel,
regardless of how noteworthy had been his earlier services to
the nation, was being influenced by illegal payoffs from the
major munitions manufacturers supplying the armed forces with
great numbers of what Colt felt were obsolescent weapons. Far
from condemning the bribery, the ominently realistic Colt
suggested to Selden that they match the bid. Selden was outraged.

I will not become a party to a negotiation with a public
officer to allow him compensation for aid in securing a
contract with Govet. The suggestion with respect to Col.
Domford is dishonorable in every way. . . .

Selden's delicate moral senses had not received their last
shock. On learning that Sam had pawned his stock of guns to
cover debts and pay for a trip to Richmond, on February 27,
1839, he wrote a stinging letter:

By what authority have you placed the property of the
Patent Arms Company in the hands of anyone and there-
upon drawn funds for your private expenditures? . . . I
know not what you may think of the morals of this business, but it seems to me not much better than putting your

hand in a man's pocket . . . if the residue is not immediately accounted for, greater difficulties may arise than you
anticipate. . . .

Colt returned to Paterson and talked the outraged Selden and
other directors out of sending him to jail.

The company had opened a store on Broadway in New York
and staffed it with a Dr. C. B. Zabriski, chemist and medical
doctor. He made an occasional sale, not enough to keep the
company going, but he made one move that was decisive in
Colt's career. He had lent one John Fuller some samples to
carry to the newly founded Republic of Texas aboard the
steamship *Charlestown,* recently bought by the Republic and
making its maiden voyage to its owners. Among the samples
were the hefty, hard-hitting five-shooter, the No. 5 pistol, later
called the Texas Paterson.

Fuller was a friend of the Republic's second President, Mirabeau Buonaparte Lamar. More than that, the President's secretary was James Colt, Sam's younger brother.

Agents of the Hackett breechloader, the army regulation Hall
musket, and even of the suicidal Cochran magazine loader were
already on the scene. But Fuller had marvelous connections, including Colonel George W. Hockley, Secretary of War under
Sam Houston (the first President) and chief ordnance officer
under Lamar.

In April 1839 Fuller wrote Paterson a letter saying:

. . . Col. Hockley has always been decidedly in favor of
the old-fashioned muskets and pistols, but I staggered his
opinion and faith I believe for the first time by showing the
superiority of the "Colt's Patent." . . .

I saw President Lamar . . . and he said he should order

a sufficient number of carbines to arm a regiment of Rangers which would be about 850. . . .

The Navy Department . . . has requested me to furnish by an order to that effect to E. W. Moore, commodore of the Texian Fleet, 180 carbines, and 180 belt pistols, 8 inch barrels. . . .

He enclosed a copy of the order from Memucan Hunt, Secretary of the Navy, to Captain E. W. Moore, commanding the Texas Navy, that confirmed Fuller's uplifting letter but added an ominous note:

The Government will not be able to pay for these articles until it effect a loan, but ten per cent. interest per annum will be allowed on all purchases until paid.

Captain Moore sailed on the steamship *Zavela* with Fuller, stopped off in Baltimore to inspect the vessels under construction for the Texas Navy, and proceeded to the Broadway shop, where, on August 3, 1839, he supervised shipping of a lot of fifty pistols and fifty carbines with all accessories and spare parts.

Further orders followed, some placed by Texans of questionable authority and all financed by a bewildering exchange of drafts and deferred payments worthy of the Byzantine treasury.

Though the American military still held back, not only the Texans but the public in general showed increasing enthusiasm for Colt's arms. In fact, a reporter for the Louisville *Journal* was so carried away he reported a Colt rifle that fired sixteen times and a pistol ten times without reloading (undoubtedly a business of replacing spent cylinders with spare charged cylinders). He said he had seen a ball shot clean through a chicken from several yards away, though it was propelled by the "explosive power of the cap alone with a single kernel of powder."

On June 29, 1840, Pliny Lawton wrote Sam that the directors had stopped production and laid off half the workmen, retaining the other half only to finish the incompleted pieces on hand.

Since the plant never started up again, the tally sheet of that date is a good summary of total production of the Paterson Patent Arms Manufacturing Company of New Jersey. Of rifles and carbines, 1,312; of pistols 2,700, about one thousand of those the hard-hitting No. 5, universally dubbed the Texas Paterson. The tally shows only 165 shotguns.

About the same time, Mighill Nutting, of Maine, turned up with a repeating rifle that a board of officers found at least the equal of Colt's and in some ways superior. Colt did not hesitate to suggest inviting Nutting to demonstrate his arm to the Paterson stockholders, then throwing him into prison on some pretext or other, "patent infringement" being a handy charge. Imprisonment in New Jersey Colt thought a splendid idea, because Nutting was a stranger there, hence presumably without influence. Cooler heads prevailed.

Nutting offered the Paterson Company a deal:

> I have been induced in the spirit of compromise to make you the following proposition as a quietus to the whole matter viz. I will sell for $12,000 all the right and title granted to me. . . .

Lawton wrote Colt he did not consider the Nutting weapon an infringement but added that the company "will endeavour to friten him. . . ."

For whatever reason, at this point Nutting and his repeating rifle disappear forever from view.

Colt's staunchest supporter suffered a tragic setback in Florida. To pacify the Spanish Indians, as the southernmost bands were called because of their centuries-old trade with Cuba, the Army set up a trading post ten miles upstream from the mouth of the Caloosahatchee River. As a guard for the operation, Colonel Harney and twenty-eight dragoons pitched tents on the bank, opposite the camp of about one hundred supposedly friendly Indians. Midstream was anchored a trading sloop. Colonel Harney's tent stood a little distance apart from those of the men.

Just before dawn on July 23, 1839, he heard firing and saw several of his men swimming in the river with Indians firing on them from the banks.

Clearly, his detachment had been surprised and the fight was over before it started. Colonel Harney fled downstream, his clothes smeared with mud as camouflage. He was searching for a canoe he had hidden six miles away when he heard somebody coming down the trail from the direction of the surprised camp. Determined to overpower his pursuer and seize his weapons, the officer hid behind a palmetto. Just before clubbing the other, Colonel Harney recognized his own orderly.

The two hailed the sloop cruising the river looking for survivors and found twelve other dragoons aboard. They reported with anger that Sergeant Bigelow had also escaped into the river but had been talked into going ashore by Chief Billy Bowlegs, an old friend, who nevertheless did not hesitate to kill the sergeant on his first step ashore.

Reaching the mouth of the river, Colonel Harney picked up a small force he had left to guard some Spanish prisoners he had caught selling arms to the Indians. The next night, they returned to the massacre site to see if they could pick up more survivors. They found one dragoon's body floating in the river and

eight ashore, all with eyes plucked out. The Indians had sacked
the trading post; the dragoons' Colt rifles were gone.

It was the first report of conflict with Indians from the extreme South. Colonel Harney, understandably, harbored a special desire to exercise his repeaters on them at another meeting.

At the other frontier, in Texas, though highly pleased with
their Colts, Texans had complained that mounted men could
not reload on horseback, because the old model required removal of the barrel to ram home charges. On August 29, 1839,
Colt received a patent for a pistol with a stronger frame, a visible trigger and trigger guard, and—most important—a lever
rammer fixed so that the cylinder could be recharged without
removing the barrel.

In December 1839, Colt wrote to a congressman that Commodore Moore had appeared in New York with money to "pay
for all the arms the Texan government have had of us and all
other arms that we can finish before he again sails."

Civilian sales must have picked up also, for the New York
Enquirer of January 24, 1840, reported that ". . . scarcely a
vessel goes to sea that the captain does not provide himself with
this means of protection against *mutiny*."

A navy board tested Colt's arms and made a report distinguished even among the other stupidities of military history by
its baffling inner contradictions.

The Colt rifle was indeed loaded and discharged of sixteen
shots (two cylinders) in two minutes, forty-nine seconds, the
report admitted. It fired an already loaded eight-shot cylinder in
twelve seconds. The rifle lay underwater for a period with no
effect on its rate of fire. Loose powder poured over the chambers came through the firing unburnt. Every feature of safety
and celerity of fire was as the inventor claimed.

Nevertheless, the board found that the repeater would suffer "greater liability to derangement and accidents when used by unskilful persons in the hurry and confusion of boarding or repelling boarders; when, after the first discharge of firearms, bayonets, pikes and cutlasses are usually and mainly relied on."

Here again that myopic look backward to the past, that refusal to accept a murderously effective new weapon because lesser weapons had sufficed in the past. And the argument that the revolvers would be used by "unskilful persons" could hardly have sat well with the U. S. Marines, who would be chiefly charged with their use.

Worse, the officers continued with an assessment of the weapons that in their own words made the first half of their report sound as silly as it was.

Every vessel of war should be armed with enough Colt rifles and pistols for boat expeditions, the board said, because of their resistance to water damage and because, further, "the facility with which they may be loaded or their receivers shifted when their possessor is even lying down in the bottom of his boat, would always . . . give them an *incalculable advantage* over other arms now used in the service."

In disgust, the Washington *Globe* of June 13, 1840, sneered at the backwardness of the military and likened them to French Canadian farmers who clung to the plow used during the reign of Louis XIV.

The editorial suggested:

There is one test, we think, which would soon decide every officer in giving a preference to the repeating gun. If any of them should ever be engaged to meet in single combat, and his antagonist should apprise him that he will come armed with one of Colt's rifle pistols, taking his station at forty yards, then to advance and fire *ad libitum,* the friend of the old system, we think, would hesitate to meet the encounter with a single duelling pistol, against one of Colt's.

The persistent resistance of the military brass did not extend to the civilian commander in chief, for President Martin Van Buren, according to the New York *Weekly Herald* of July 18, 1840, sent as a gift to Seyd Seyd Bin Sultan Bin Ahmed, the Imam of Muscat, four Colt pistols and two rifles, the pistols five-shooters and "the most magnificent we ever saw, and would grace the belt of any monarch."

In far-off Florida the dreary war dragged on. The Spanish Indians under Chekika struck again. On August 7, 1840, they raided Indian Key, where the distinguished botanist Dr. Henry Perrine was experimenting with introduction of tropical plants to Florida's agriculture. They killed the scientist and six others; Dr. Perrine's family escaped by hiding in a turtle crawl.

With great enthusiasm, Colonel Harney accepted the mission of rooting the Spanish Indians out of the Everglades. On December 4, 1840, with ninety men in sixteen canoes, he entered the swamp on Chekika's trail.

By the end of December 1840, the metropolitan newspapers of the Eastern Seaboard carried exultant accounts of Colonel Harney's meeting with Chekika.

A correspondent aboard the brig *Wakulla* wrote the Tallahassee *Floridian:*

> Col. Harney . . . with a force of about 90 men entered the everglades in canoes, guided by John, a negro who was captured by the Indians in 1835. . . . The negro conducted the colonel through the everglades to the Indian town, and he surrounded it and fired upon them, killing one or two Indians and taking thirty eight prisoners. In the

assault, the chief of the band, Chai-ki-ka, escaped, and was pursued several miles by one of the dragoons, and overtaken and shot. Among the prisoners taken were ten warriors, nine of whom were hung; the life of the tenth being saved for a future guide.

The colonel recaptured thirteen or fourteen of the Colt's rifles, taken from him at Caloosahatchee by the Indians, and about two thousand dollars worth of goods carried off by the Indians from Indian Key.

In St. Augustine, to celebrate the death of Chekika, the paper reported, "Our market is illuminated to-night—the big gun is out—the band is playing cheerfully; and the people are shouting for joy."

An editorial in a New York paper urged arming two regiments of dragoons with carbines immediately, and added:

> We see no reason why these arms are not as applicable to the Infantry as to Dragoon Service; in fact they seem indispensable for the termination of our Indian wars. On all occasions where our brave little forces have met the Indian forces in Florida, he has made his escape before they could reload their muskets after the first discharge. With Colts repeating arms our men can pursue the enemy until each has fired six in lieu of one round, without stopping to reload.

Colonel Harney himself wrote Colt in answer to his inquiry about the record his rifles had made against the Seminoles:

> . . . They have surpassed my expectations (which were great). . . . It is my honest opinion that no other guns than those of your invention will be used in a few years.

First Sergeant P. W. Henry, of the 2d Dragoons, wrote a more detailed and even more glowing endorsement:

> . . . there was not a man in the whole detachment that did not feel himself of five times the force with one of your *repeaters,* than with the common carbine or musket. And so eager were the soldiers to get each one of your rifles, and so great was the desire to be attached to this select corps, that to receive one of your patent arms was the reward of every good and brave soldier.

The sergeant registered a mild complaint about the variety of calibers but added:

> In passing through the Indian country, I always felt myself safer with one of your rifles in my hands, than if I was attended by a body of ten or fifteen men armed with the common musket or carbine. . . .

He gave in detail target accuracy, rate of fire, and penetration tests, and concluded,

> Your rifle must and will shortly supersede the carbine and musket now used in the army; and, when that is done, it may be considered that the efficiency of the army is increased in a tenfold degree.

A letter to the *Evening Star* on January 16, 1841, divided its honors between Colonel Harney and the Colt rifle:

> It is Colonel Harney alone, with less than one hundred men armed with Colt's Patent Repeating Rifles carrying sixteen charges each, who has reached the haunts of the savage foe, . . . far beyond all former penetration of the white man—and to Colonel Harney and his brave followers

alone is due all the credit of the present favorable aspect of affairs in Florida.

More than two years ago Colonel Harney visited the President of the United States and the Secretary of War . . . and volunteered himself, with such a disposition of the troops, to arm 500 men with Colt's repeating rifles, and never leave the everglades while there was a living Indian there.

The article concludes with dark hints of election-year shenanigans for diverting dollars where they would buy votes instead of effective weapons, namely Colt repeaters.

The force of the letter is somewhat diluted on learning it was written by Sam Colt himself.

Reports from further military testing began to take on a new tone. Newspapers quoted an army officer after tests on the steam frigate *Fulton:* "There are no men on earth who could withstand a shock from a hundred others with such arms in their hands."

Even the Navy, which a few weeks before had said the repeaters were not useful for "unskilful persons" in boarding engagements, reported after the *Fulton* demonstration: ". . . we believe it would be next to impossible to board a ship where Colt's arms were used by the marines and small-arm men."

At the Sandy Hook gunnery-practice station, a party of marines armed with flintlocks and another with Colt rifles laid down rapid fire for ten minutes. The report said the fire of flintlocks "appeared unsustained and feeble in comparison"; and "upon inspection of the target it was so completely riddled [by the Colt rifles] as to justify the opinion that no body of men could advance under similar fire."

In contradiction to the preposterous earlier navy report on

the uselessness of repeaters in boarding actions, the *Fulton* report continued:

> . . . in boarding or repelling boarders, or, in fact, in almost any case in which small arms are resorted to in sea-fights, a rapid and well-sustained fire at the onset is everything.
>
> There being six, and, with a very slight interruption, twelve discharges to make instead of two, it is to be presumed that very few instances would occur of close struggle which would not be decided before it should become necessary to reload at all.
>
> Signed by Andrew Harwood, Lieutenant, U. S. Navy.

Nevertheless, the U.S. armed forces were not buying any. And one John Ehlers had become treasurer of the Patent Arms Company and added his nagging voice to Selden's in deploring Sam's sales tactics and expense accounts. Ehlers quietly acquired three hundred shares and enough proxies to control the company.

VI

Despite the troubles of the Patent Arms Company and his exhausting efforts to persuade a reluctant military to adopt his arms, Colt somehow found the energy to acquire a new obsession. He designed a submarine mine system that he believed made other harbor defenses obsolete.

Colt took himself one more weary time to Washington and installed himself as usual at Fuller's Hotel, an establishment considered the ultimate in chic by Americans but the object of the caustic wit of Charles Dickens in his account of his voyages in America.

On June 19, 1841, Colt wrote President John Tyler:

It is with a little diffidence that I venture to submit the following for your consideration; feeling as I do that its apparent extravagance may prevent you from paying it that attention which it merits and but for the duty I owe my country in these threatening times, I should still longer delay making this communication.

There seems to prevail at this time with all parties a sense of the importance of effectually protecting our Sea Coast; and as economy is a primary consideration in the present exhausted state of our treasury I think I have a right to expect a favorable consideration of the propositions which I have determined to make. For more than five years past I have employed my leisure, in study, & experiment, to perfect the invention of which I now consider myself master; & which if adopted for the service of our government, will not only save them millions in outlay for the construction of means of defence, but in the event of foreign war it will prove a perfect safeguard against all the combined fleets of Europe without exposing the life of our citizens.

Colt cited the experiments of Robert Fulton decades earlier. Fulton's experiments failed because of faulty control over his mines, but they did demonstrate the devastating effect of underwater explosions on ships' hulls. Colt reported that he had solved Fulton's problem of control:

Discoveries since Fulton's time combined with an invention original with myself, enable me to effect the instant destruction of either Ships or Steamers, at my pleasure on their entering a harbour, whether singly or in whole fleets; while those vessels to which I am disposed to allow a passage are secure from a possibility of being injured. All this I can do in perfect security and without giving an invading enemy the slightest sign of his danger.

Colt said a single man could operate his "destroying agent." Colt then got down to business. For twenty thousand dollars and a governmental helping hand he would demonstrate his engine, with the understanding that after a successful demonstration the government would pay an annual premium for his secret.

During this Washington interlude, Colt must have engaged a secretary, because the letters are noteworthy for their clean English and correct spelling, hardly Colt's strong points.

To a sympathetic Senator Samuel Southard, of New Jersey, Colt disclosed his harbor defense system, including apparently the so-called secret that made his system different from other remote-control explosive devices, a secret most scientists and military men scoffed at as non-existent.

While Senator Southard was maneuvering to have the expenses of a demonstration included in congressional naval appropriations, Colt flirted with a Russian delegation. He wrote Senator Southard that he had been invited to go to Russia aboard the steam frigate *Kamchatka,* leaving suspended in the air a thinly veiled threat to peddle his war engines to a foreign power. Colt never in his career displayed great sentimentality about his native land and frequently enough showed contempt and cynicism for the honesty and intelligence of America's foremost leaders. Also, considering the flexible patriotism of most of the arms merchants of history, Senator Southard had good reason to consider the threat more than a bluff.

Colt turned the screw down harder in a following letter:

. . . should I not meet with satisfactory encouragement from our Government, I shall avail myself of this favorable opportunity to go Abroad; therefore it is of vast importance that my case should be immediately decided, that unless some inducement should be offered for me to remain at home, I shall at once be enabled to commence preparations for my departure.

And later he wrote Senator Southard in even stronger terms:

I wish you to converse with the President, the Secretary of the Navy and the Chairman of the Naval Committee of the House of Representatives. . . . It is my wish to give my own country the exclusive use of my discovery, and nothing but actual want will induce me to seek patronage from foreign Governments.

(As it happens, the Prussian inventor Moritz Hermann von Jacobi, in the service of the Czar, had developed a system of underwater mining at least as advanced as Colt's, and so Colt could hardly have done much good for himself on a voyage to Russia.)

Senator Southard did squeeze fifty thousand dollars into the naval appropriations bill with the understanding of Secretary of the Navy George Badger that twenty thousand dollars would be earmarked for Colt's demonstration. Unfortunately, on September 10, 1841, Tyler's entire cabinet resigned (except for Secretary of State Daniel Webster), and Colt's supporters had to begin all over, persuading the new Secretary of the Navy, Abel P. Upshur, that the entire fifty thousand dollars for naval ordnance development was not a windfall to be scattered about according to his whim. Back at the Patent Arms Company, what at first appeared a stroke of luck merely widened the rupture between Colt and Ehlers.

Colonel Bomford, who had long resisted Colt arms, broke down and ordered one hundred carbines for the garrison on Governors Island, in New York Harbor. Sam asked for his commission and royalty. The new treasurer, Ehlers, said he would apply the sum to Sam's debts and advances instead of delivering the cash. Since Ehlers was a major stockholder, to some extent it meant he was putting Sam's earnings into his own pocket.

Dr. Zabriski reported with indignation from the Broadway store that he had been about to sell twenty-five No. 5 pistols to a Mexican client when Ehlers stepped in and killed the deal.

Ehlers was selling the leftover stock from the closed Paterson factory and pocketing the money. Clearly, he was intent on liquidating the company for his own profit. Colt asked the courts for an injunction forbidding further sales by Ehlers.

Colt had only part of his attention focused on Paterson, however, for he had become encouraged by the Secretary of the Navy in his mine project. In September 1841 he drew up an unchartered corporation:

Whereas I, Samuel Colt . . . have invented and discovered certain new & useful improvements for the better protection of our Harbours & Coasts, the nature of which is such that a harbour like that of New York can be defended against the whole British Navy, at less expense than the cost of one single steam ship of War. And whereas I . . . have entered into a secret arrangement with the Government of the United States in which they have agreed to furnish $20,000 towards defraying the expenses necessary to make an effective exhibition of the same, & have further promised that after they have witnessed a successful exhibition they will recommend to Congress to appropriate a sum of money for the purpose of the right to use said invention for the protection of all the harbours of the United States. . . .

Then Colt divided rights to the invention into two thousand shares worth fifty dollars each and offered half the shares for sale—but not to the public, for he warned subscribers that he would reveal only so much of his secret as they needed to know to impress them with its value:

All operations shall be kept secret and conducted under my direction. . . .

In the midst of his troubles with Ehlers and the collapse of the Paterson factory, plus his worries about the submarine mine, came a catastrophe that staggered even the usually indomitable Sam Colt.

On the New York waterfront, the master of the sailing vessel *Kalamazoo,* offended by the increasingly rank odor of a packing case consigned to New Orleans, called in police. Inside the case they found the body of Samuel Adams, a printer who had disappeared several days earlier. Police tracked down the drayman who had delivered the case. He reported he had been stopped at the corner of Chambers and Broadway and hired to carry the case from an office nearby to the ship at the foot of Maiden Lane. It was elementary police work to trace the case to the office of John Colt, Sam's eldest brother, four years his senior.

On September 23, 1841, the police arrested John Colt for murder. He insisted on his innocence. A grand jury returned a true bill. Every penny Sam could get his hands on he dedicated to his brother's defense. As attorneys, he engaged Dudley Selden and Elias Ogden. John had once worked as a clerk in Selden's office, and Ogden was representing Sam in his difficulties with John Ehlers and the Paterson Company.

The elder Colt (then thirty-one) had briefly been a U. S. Marine but apparently had a medical discharge. He suffered from what was probably tuberculosis; recurrent attacks of bleeding of the lungs drove him to move repeatedly in search of a healthful climate. He wandered the Ohio and Mississippi valleys, often as a riverboat gambler, for he had considerable skill in mathematics. Of a piece with the rakish life of a gambler, in Cincinnati he was involved with the octoroon mistress of a white planter, who challenged him to a duel. He fled on the next steamboat, but returned to Cincinnati, where he managed a museum and wrote a textbook on bookkeeping. He seems to have been the center of a racy circle. His Norwegian mistress committed suicide for unknown reasons.

In 1839 he moved to New York and opened a book-publishing venture. He lived in a smart neighborhood, at 42 Murray Street, and kept his offices at Chambers and Broadway, across from City Hall Park. Caught trying to break into a Wall Street office, he went to jail, but police charged him only with tying on a monumental drunk. He had no further police trouble till his arrest on a charge of murdering the missing printer.

John recanted his first protestation of innocence and gave his version of the tragedy.

On the afternoon of September 17, 1841, the printer had called on him to collect $71.15. John's figures showed the debt to be only $55.85. As men frequently did in those turbulent days, they resorted to fist fighting. John said Adams struck first, causing a bloody nose. In the struggle, Adams twisted John's cravat so tight that John was strangling. His hand fell on a hammer; he struck Adams on the head till the printer fell to the floor, breathed heavily for a moment, and died.

Blood had flowed in torrents from his wounds and was spreading all over the floor. I was afraid that it would seep through to the apothecary store beneath. I tried to stop it by tying my handkerchief tightly around his neck, but it didn't seem to do any good. Eventually I got a piece of cord and after taking off his stock, I tied it around his neck. . . .

John swabbed away the blood, nailed Adams into the packing case, and addressed it to a nonexistent Mr. Gross in New Orleans by way of the *Kalamazoo*. By bad luck, New York suffered an unseasonable heat wave and the boat for some reason delayed departure, leading to his downfall.

Many reporters, especially those of the New York *Sun* and the *Democratic Review*, responded to John's undoubted charm and noted that he did have some case for self-defense, for he showed bruises on his throat, and it was Adams, after all, who had come seeking a quarrel with Colt, not the other way around. The dead printer apparently had a bad name as a bully and was hard pressed for money, so John's story of the victim's initial attack was plausible. Nevertheless, John was in jail and ordered to stand trial in January 1842.

Some hostile newspapers openly doubted whether the brother of a famed inventor, supposedly a wealthy man, would be found guilty. Those reporters had never had a glance into Sam's bankbook; he was probably considerably less wealthy than the poorest of the hostile writers.

At this point enters, or rather, re-enters, an astonishing character.

Since Sam's marriage to the beautiful German girl with the improbable English name of Caroline Henshaw, she had faded out of his public life. From their ocean crossing to John's trial, a span of six years, her name is nowhere mentioned. While in Philadelphia on business, John supposedly picked up by hazard a beautiful young girl named Caroline Henshaw. In January 1841 he took her home, installed her as the mistress of his household, and taught her to read and write.

Caroline was soon pregnant. When the child was born, shortly after John's arrest for murder, eyebrows shot up, for Caroline named the boy Samuel Colt, Jr. (When Sam took over responsibility for the boy's upbringing, Sam renamed him Samuel Caldwell Colt and pointedly dropped the "Jr." Nevertheless, when he referred to the boy in writing, he often archly enclosed "my nephew" in quotation marks, a kind of written poke of the elbow in the ribs and knowing wink.)

During the lengthy trial, Sam engaged himself feverishly in the submarine mine project, counting on stock sales and the promised government support for funds to prop up John's defense. On October 9, 1841, he wrote the Secretary of the Navy:

> Circumstances of a nature too painful to relate have rendered it of vital importance that I should raise a som of money at once.

On October 16, 1841, Sam, in the company of Captain A. V. Fraser on the revenue cutter *Wolcott,* surveyed the Narrows to lay out a defense that would protect the port "against the whole British Navy" with only one man to operate the battery. He presented his plan to the collector of the port, Edward Curtis. Captain Fraser reported the collector's indifference to Colt's startling claims with a classic description of the comfortable and stupid bureaucrat triumphant:

> My "Captain," as Titus can tell you, is one who is terribly inconvenienced by anything which interferes in the most remote manner with the monotony of his life. . . .

Money trickled in from submarine-mine stock sales to friends who may well have been tactfully using that device to cover charitable donations for John's defense.

Major William Gibbs McNeill, of the Topographic Engineers, had become a supporter of Colt's project, and as a former army engineer of great reputation, he had some influence in Washington. He wrote Colt a letter of introduction to the new Secretary of the Navy, Upshur.

Back to Washington and Fuller's Hotel.

Mr. Upshur sent a messenger for Sam, and in private session Sam disclosed the secret of his underwater battery.

On November 24, 1841, Colt wrote Upshur a letter confirming their private agreement.

> Agreeably to your wish I will proceed at once in my preparations for the exhibition of my Submarine Battery on the scale suggested by you though I hope you may yet be induced to furnish me facilities to test my invention on the scale originally intended.

The last reference to a larger-scale test was his wistful rebuke to Upshur for vetoing a scheme to blow up a whole fleet and the entire fifty-thousand-dollar special appropriation in one blast. Upshur advanced Colt only six thousand dollars.

On December 18, 1841, the submarine mine company published a list of stockholders, among them George W. Whistler, whose son became the famed artist (for that reason, George inevitably became known to history as "Whistler's father").

Meanwhile, because the court had not acted on Sam's plea for injunction, John Ehlers was busily peddling the Patent Arms Company inventory for his own account. Among his customers was Commodore Thomas Catesby Jones, who in December 1841 bought one hundred carbines and one hundred No. 5 pistols for the Pacific Squadron. Shortly afterward, the New Jersey court issued an injunction against further sales by Ehlers of the Paterson stores of arms.

The first part of 1842 was a trying time for Sam. John Ehlers advertised a meeting for January 11, 1842, to dispose of all the goods and chattels of the Paterson Works and dissolve its affairs and very existence; John's trial began on January 18, 1842.

As it will, fate continued to kick the man while he was down. On February 8, 1842, his stoutest defenders in the military failed him by sending him a letter from Florida complaining of his repeaters and recommending that they no longer be issued.

> Mr. Samuel Colt
>
> Sir: I am very sorry to say that your arms have proved an entire failure when put to the test of actual service. Lieut Sloan Comdg the Marines on the 13th Jany addressed me as follows: "I would respectfully suggest that Colts firearms be no longer used in my command."
>
> Signed by Captain McLaughlan, U. S. Marine Corps.

The marine captain reported several accidents: burst cylinders and barrels, jammed cap primers. He generously added a kinder note:

> I am perfectly satisfied that the principle of these arms is a good one and that they can be made the invaluable weapon they now pretend to be—but to effect this they must be made with a degree of attention and care which was sadly deficient in these.

McLaughlan's formal report to the Navy Department included the news of the death of one marine, killed by a bursting cylinder.

Again the marine officer defended Colt's reputation as an inventor:

> Upon the whole I attribute the failure of the Arms to meet the most sanguine expectation of the inventor, to the infamous manner of their manufacture rather than to any organic defect in the principles of their construction. . . .

He even added an invaluable note contradicting the monotonously repeated objection of high brass in rejecting Colt's arms:

> The objection so prevalent and so constantly used against them that their complex or difficult construction render them more liable to injury and more difficult to keep in order . . . has proved an imaginary one.

Colt plunged through the loophole offered by the captain and whipped off a letter to Commodore Lewis Warrington, president of the Board of Navy Commissioners:

> The chancery suit part of the wrangling over the dissolution of the Patent Arms Company . . . I am fearful, had induced Ehlers to furnish to Government Arms imperfectly manufactured for the purpose of injuring their sail when they shall again come under my control.

Sam also wrote his attorney a letter explaining exactly the technique of metallurgic sabotage he accused Ehlers of resorting to as a guarantee of bankruptcy so that the company's assets would fall to him through a forced sale.

To cap his troubles, in June 1842 the Navy stopped honoring his drafts for the submarine mine.

At Castle Clinton, on the lower Manhattan shore, was an open-air pleasure palace called Niblo's Castle Garden. Mr. Niblo made an agreement with the hard-pressed Sam to split the gate from a demonstration of his mine in the waters visible from the garden. Ever the showman, Sam picked the Fourth of July, 1842, thirteenth anniversary of the Ware Pond explosion, for his immensely more ambitious fireworks.

On the great day, the mayor, city council, and thousands of spectators attended, and reporters were there from twelve major publications. The skipper of the Navy brig *Washington* invited Colt to touch off the explosion from his craft, but Colt accepted instead the invitation of Captain Francis Gregory, of the more prestigious, 74-gunner, the *North Carolina.*

According to the New York *Evening Post:*

An old hulk was moored off Castle Garden fitted with temporary masts, from which were displayed various flags, with piratical devices, immediately under which the battery was placed, and the effect of the explosions was tremendous. The vessel was shattered into fragments, some of which were thrown two or three hundred feet in the air, and there was not a single piece left longer than a man could have carried in one hand.

Colt himself wrote Upshur:

Immediately after the national salute was fired at 12 o'clock yesterday I made an experiment with my submarine battery . . . on a vessil about one hundred tons which was being towed through the water at the rate of about three nots an hour. . . .

That last note, about destroying a moving vessel, was critical. Underwater explosions had become commonplace in England, where Royal Navy engineers routinely removed sunken hulks from navigation channels by blowing them out of the way. The trick that held up use of mines as harbor defenses was setting them off at the critical moment when the target vessel was moving exactly over the planted engine.

The New York *Herald* confirmed that the hulk had been moving when destroyed:

> The battery having been placed under her bottom the cable of the doomed vessel was cut, & when by the aid of the tide and the boats of the United States' Ship *North Carolina,* her speed through the water had been made about four knots an hour, the explosion took place.

But even that favorable account notes that the charge had been carefully placed where it would do the most damage, an impossibility against a free-sailing enemy fleet. Scholars who have studied Colt's methods do not entirely discredit rumors that he fixed the charge directly to the hull and fired it with a conveniently long cable so that he would appear to have touched off the explosion exactly when the hulk passed over the mine.

The New York *Sun* expressed qualified admiration:

> Any thing less than a ship of the line must have been either destroyed or capsized had the explosion taken place immediately under it. But it strikes us that the great difficulty in rendering the battery efficient must be the impossibility of placing it immediately under any vessel that it may be designed to destroy.

Upshur seemed impressed by reports of the Castle Garden show, though some officers were dubious about using Navy Department advances to finance a beer-garden spectacular. They probably did not even suspect Sam was diverting some submarine-mine money to his brother's defense fund.

Repeatedly, Sam had indicated that the enemy he would defend America's harbors against was the British Navy, for Great Britain and the United States were quarreling about the New Brunswick-Maine border; a few hotheads talked about war. But in July 1842 negotiations settled the dispute. Even the seemingly endless Seminole War was winding down. On the very day, August 20, 1842, scheduled for a second demonstration, this time in the Potomac River at Washington, the Senate ratified the treaty that settled the border trouble.

For the second demonstration, this time before a meager eight thousand spectators, Colt posted a sixty-ton clam boat off Greenfield Point, where now stands the National War College. *Niles National Register* reported:

> . . . the steamer containing the President and members of the cabinet, with their suites, was opposite the spectators and its illustrious and precious freight received a very hearty greeting from the mouths of twenty-four guns. A few minutes afterwards the signal for the explosion was given by the discharge of a twenty-four pounder, and instantaneously, as though a missile from the gun itself had borne the torch to a magazine in her, the old craft was sent in ten millions of fragments five hundred feet into the air, and then fell into the water with a roar like that of Niagara.

Colt's precise position at the time of the explosion, even the placing of the mine and the means of detonating it, remain unknown to this day. He said that he fired the shot from Alexandria, five miles away; "the noise of my explosion and the report of the signal gun was blended together in one sound." Colt could well have been stationed in the old Armory only a few feet from the explosion, and many experts think he was.

Colt's ferocious defense of his secret, including that improbable story that he was five miles off, worked against him in military circles. And somehow he had made an enemy of John Quincy Adams, once President of the United States and then a venerable power in the House of Representatives. Among other objections, Adams raised the curious argument that he was "opposed to blowing up ships of war with submarine batteries; . . . it should be done by fair and honest warfare."

Still avoiding the professional military, who had always disappointed him, Sam proposed another public dazzler of a test against a moving vessel, this time for the benefit of a fair sponsored by the American Institute. Secretary Upshur informed the Institute that the Navy did not intend for its experiments to be exploited commercially (echoes of the Niblo's Castle Garden fireworks).

The last week of September, 1842, delivered Sam a double blow.

On September 27, 1842, Secretary Upshur wrote Sam a brusque note that showed waning support for the mine project.

On the same day, a New York jury found John Colt guilty of murder in the first degree. He was sentenced to hang on November 18, 1842. The stunned defendant made an intemperate speech that turned much of the hitherto sympathetic public against him.

Secretary Upshur apparently harbored some personal sympathy for Sam, however, for he visited the distressed inventor two days later and granted permission for the American Institute demonstration.

While Colt was preoccupied with his underwater mines, on September 30, 1842, John Ehlers made history of a sort by selling to himself for six thousand dollars the machinery and unassembled gun parts of the Patent Arms Company, putting it out of existence forever.

Colt could soothe his injured soul with a showman's delight in the popular success of his well-publicized third mine shot. On October 18, 1842, more than forty thousand spectators lined the shore. All the navy and army officers in town, plus the Secretary of War, John C. Spencer, came aboard the *North Carolina* to witness the demonstration. Colt characteristically slipped away from reporters and professional observers to make his shot in secret.

Aboard the revenue cutter *Ewing,* anchored off the Battery, he touched off a mine under the 260-ton brig *Volta,* appropriately named after the Italian physicist who had developed the electrical science that led to the ship's undoing.

Niles National Register reported:

> . . . the great bulk seemed lifted by some unseen power, the bow and stern sunk heavily, and the whole was enveloped by a huge pile of dense mist, some two hundred feet in diameter and about eighty high, through which now and then were seen pieces of timber, of which even the shape could not be guessed.

A spectacular show for the Institute's fair, but there is no evidence the brig was moving, and so it was just another underwater explosion much like the two previous that had not convinced the military of the value of Sam's secret.

John Colt's execution day lay only a month beyond the American Institute show. John waited in a death cell that friends had transformed into a fashionable parlor. (He had not seen Caroline since the trial.) Among the friends he received in his cozy cell, incidentally, was John Howard Payne, author of "Home, Sweet Home." Another visitor reported vases with flowers, a caged canary, bookshelves hanging from silken cords, paintings, and a fine rug.

Charles A. Dana, after a visit to the cell, wrote:

Colt, in an elegant dressing gown lolls in a patent extension chair, smoking an aromatic Havana. . . . His lunch-
eon brought in from an hotel consists of quail on toast,
game pates, reed birds, ortolans, fowl, vegetables, coffee,
cognac.

Nevertheless, November 18, 1842, inexorably approached.
Colt's appeal failed. Though smart money in the street was bet-
ting he would never hang, Colt's future seemed short. Rumors
flew about that mysterious agents were offering bribes to prison
officials.

The sheriff granted John's request to put off the hanging till
4 P.M. John wanted the extra time to "make an honest woman"
of Caroline, as the expression of the day went. At noon of execution day, Caroline and a small wedding party repaired to
John's cell, where the Reverend Dr. Henry Athon, rector of
St. Mark's Church, married the couple.

Assisting at the macabre ceremony was Sam Colt, which
raises questions.

Was the bride indeed the same Caroline Henshaw he had
brought back from Scotland? The identity of name and age
seem to admit no other possibility—especially in view of the
breath-takingly candid "Jr." Caroline had affixed to her son's
name, inescapably pointing a finger at the true father.

Well, then, had he really married Caroline Henshaw in Scotland?

If so, had he divorced her? Where and when?

If he had not, what was he doing witnessing her bigamous
marriage—and to a man about to hang? What advantage was
there for her to be known as the widow of a hanged murderer,
rather than as the errant wife of a respected industrialist? (At

the probate of Sam Colt's will, in 1863, Samuel Caldwell Colt produced a marriage license proving Colt had married Caroline in Scotland.)

Even stranger events were coming.

Immediately after the ceremony, the couple was granted an hour's conjugal visit. Then began a series of comings and goings and bizarre mishaps that posed a mystery that has never been solved.

The sheriff admitted several attempts at bribing him to permit the prisoner's escape. He even accepted one thousand dollars that he later surrendered. About ten thousand spectators who had gathered in the street to witness the hanging noticed a closed carriage parked near a side door. A stream of defense lawyers and friends visited the cell. Shortly after 2 P.M. John said good-by to Lewis Gaylord Clarke, John Howard Payne, Sam Colt, and Caroline. They left the cell together, Caroline with head bent, her face concealed behind a handkerchief, for she was weeping.

At 3:55 P.M. the Reverend Dr. Athon started toward the cell with the sheriff to get Colt. At that same instant, the cupola of the Tombs burst into flames.

The five hundred official witnesses within the courtyard milled about and were joined by prisoners released to prevent their death should the fire spread. Gates opened for the fire equipment, and many in the courtyard fled outside, certainly some of the released prisoners among them.

The fire was not extinguished till after sunset; the crowd noted that the sentence specifically directed that the execution take place "between sunup and sundown." John's execution would no longer be legal, Philadelphia lawyers among the spectators argued.

The question was moot.

On returning to the death cell, the sheriff reported that John Colt was stretched dead on his cot, a butcher knife plunged into his chest. A hastily summoned coroner's jury ruled suicide, reportedly without viewing the body, though that lapse in procedure made little difference, since none of the jurors had ever seen John and so could not have identified his body.

Those who had argued that the brother of a supposedly wealthy and influential man like Sam Colt would never hang came up with a bouquet of bizarre plots. The most widely accepted was that the body of the supposed suicide was a cadaver from a medical school substituted for John during the confusion of the fire. Many believed it was John who left the cell, in Caroline's clothes. Even the least suspicious spectators wondered about the disappearance of the mysterious carriage during the fire, and about the fact that the Colts had made no funeral arrangements.

For the next several years reports trickled in that John Colt had been seen alive in widely separated parts of the globe, but no evidence exists that he survived that grisly afternoon.

Shortly afterward, Caroline and her baby left for Europe.

For weeks, Sam performed experiments at New York University to perfect the efficacy of his detonating spark. In nearby quarters, the celebrated painter and inventor Samuel F. B. Morse was perfecting his telegraph. The two inventors became close friends—collaborators to some extent, for both their devices depended on long-range transmission of electrical impulses. The two inventors, both lodged at New York University, had swapped reels of insulated wire to make possible several public demonstrations of their separate inventions. Colt prepared enough telegraph wire to stretch forty miles, from Washington to Baltimore.

Again Sam's family intruded on his many other troubles. His

younger brother, James, had gone west to St. Louis and frequently wrote Sam letters so affectionate as to border on the mawkish. James became embroiled in a quarrel over a Mrs. Wilson, whose younger brother, John Burr, challenged him to a duel.

The pair met at dawn on the Illinois bank. The procedure was for the two to hold their pistols at their sides, raise them at the signal "Fire," and shoot any time during a count of three. James missed his shot, Burr hit James in the right leg. The court sentenced James to ten days in jail. James had worried that the duel would hurt his political ambitions, but the unpredictable public apparently endowed him with a romantic glamour.

On November 9, 1843, at Wood's Hole, Massachusetts, Sam found a bark, the *Brunette,* that seemed suitably dilapidated for his test because the crew had mutinied rather than continue sailing it. The bark sailed for Washington, where Sam planned to lift it off the Potomac with an astonishing 150 barrels of gunpowder.

On the side, Colt had been pushing another invention, cartridges wrapped in tinfoil instead of paper. They resisted deterioration of the enclosed powder by exposure to moisture, a serious problem with paper cartridges of the time. Those tests he supervised personally, from rolling of the cartridges through to their explosion, demonstrated a spectacular superiority over existent cartridges. Those tests performed on tinfoil cartridges that had been out of his sight failed because they had been sabotaged, sometimes so crudely as to show open punctures made with a knife blade. After several tests with mixed results, the government placed a large order but never went through with the deal. Colt abandoned the enterprise in December 1843 to pursue his obsession with the submarine mine.

Another ordnance demonstration that went wrong through no fault of his dealt Colt's plans a serious blow. On February 28, 1844, aboard the new steam frigate *Princeton,* President Tyler and a large party of political and military dignitaries gathered to witness the firing of a twelve-inch cannon dubbed the Peacemaker. The cannon burst. Flying shrapnel narrowly missed the President and killed five in his party, among them Abel Upshur, who was then Secretary of State, and Thomas W. Gilmer, newly appointed Secretary of the Navy. Upshur's death removed from the government the one man who knew the secret of Colt's mine system. (Senator Southard had died weeks before.)

Though the Peacemaker accident had killed his most powerful and sympathetic supporter, Colt bored ahead, for the international situation had warmed up again with pressure from the Republic of Texas for annexation as one of the United States. The United States Government was nervous about Mexican reaction if its errant province joined the Union and even more nervous that a rebuffed Texas would enter an alliance with Great Britain and, as an independent nation, give the British a foothold in the Southwest. Defense projects naturally flourish during tense times.

For his fourth demonstration, early in April 1844, Colt sowed his mines on the Anacostia River bottom between the Old Arsenal at Greenfield Point and the navy yard.

There is some suspicion that Colt himself wrote or at least edited several newspaper stories covering the event. From one of those stories:

> . . . the whole populace was in a fidget of satisfaction and impatience—everybody in every place, from the halls of Congress and the Executive Departments down to the

boarding house kitchen and bootblacks' cellars, were hurrying through the business of the morning to ensure an early dinner and a sight of *the blow up.*

A Lieutenant Junius Boyle had volunteered to sail the *Brunette,* renamed the *Styx* for its death cruise, into the mine field. He and his crew had agreed to jump ship in a boat and fire a rocket when clear of danger. The schedule called for blowing up of the ship while under full sail, at exactly 5 P.M. At 5:10 P.M. another explosion would clear the channel. In the following minutes other explosions were to follow, apparently to discharge in the safest manner all the explosives that remained in the channel.

As is usual with most one-shot operations, the scheme went wildly agley.

A reporter who signed himself Sigma and who may well have been Sam Colt wrote an account for the Washington *Daily National Intelligencer* (later reprinted in Colt's home-town Hartford *Courant*).

I strolled down to the shores of the Eastern Branch about three o'clock; yet though it was more than an hour before the appointed time, I found thousands there before me, patiently waiting (under no very merciful sun, either) the destined hour to arrive. Stationing myself on an elevated bluff, I enjoyed, in delighted silence, the panorama which surrounded me. Close by, the wharves and river beach, covered with people; the nearer heights covered with carriages and vehicles of every description, with riders on horseback, companies of children, and anxious mothers trying to restrain them from venturing to the precipices; below, the placid blue stream. . . .

In the middle of the stream, and in full view, lay the object on which all eyes were fastened—a ship of about five hundred tons, very old, but newly painted, black with a white streak, her sails much patched and weather beaten, having at her mainmast head a red flag, and at the mizzen mast the American ensign floating beautifully in the breeze. She was at anchor, and near her were boats that seemed, from their motions, to be in communication with those on board. Presently a steamboat heaved in view and, taking her station at a convenient distance, began to let off steam; and before long, another and longer appeared, having her deck black with a crowd of people and bearing the national colors, having as it was understood, the President on board, accompanied by the Heads of Departments and other officers of Government.

As all were now waiting with much impatience, a gun was heard from the navy yard, which was followed by others, till a salute of seventeen guns was fired. We now began to hope that the play had begun. Every eye was turned towards the ship; but she did not move. A little boat advanced and removed certain buoys which had been floating near the spot where the battery lay; and soon after a low and peculiar sound was heard, when a most beautiful jet, of mingled water, fire and smoke, rose to a considerable height near the opposite shore, and as the water fell back in white translucent masses, the smoke, colored by the sun's rays with all the dyes of the prism, slowly melted into the air, while the grains of wet powder, ignited and smoking, fell in soft showers upon the bright surface of the river. This exhibition . . . seemed intended as a sort of prelude. . . .

The master showman had overcome the inventor. He could not resist a few theatrical blank shots to warm up the house.

At length the American ensign was lowered, and the few persons on board the ship [*Styx*], passing over her side, were rowed off, amid the huzzas which rose from the shores, and the vessel, abandoned to the breeze, commenced her fateful voyage. She proceeded slowly, and as steadily as if navigated by the most skilful crew. As she approached the spot where the buoys had floated, an explosion took place, and the water was thrown up in a pyramid, but a few yards ahead of her. "Ah!" exclaimed a thousand tongues, "what a pity! it was a failure after all!" The ship held on her course, and in a few minutes another mountain of water, larger and blacker than the first, rose on her larboard bow, and so close to her that she rocked under the undulation. "Oh, he has missed her! but it was very near." The words were scarcely uttered when a third explosion took place—the bows and bowsprit of the ship, instantly shattered to atoms, were thrown into the air. The fore part of the vessel was lifted up almost out of the water, and then immediately sank, while the stern continued above water, and the mizzenmast was left still standing, though in an inclined position. The spars and sails hung in confusion, being suddenly blackened by the smoke, and the whole presenting a wreck in the highest degree picturesque. . . . There was no accident, no injury, no disappointment in any respect; the public expectation was not only met but surpassed; and when the boat containing the crew darted swiftly to the wreck, and with some difficulty restored the stripes and stars to their former station, it required no stretch of the imagination to

fancy that we beheld a captive invader, which had been
compelled to strike, and was now taken possession of as
lawful prize.

One reporter sounded a sour note:

It would seem that the explosion was made a little too
soon, as, had the battery struck the vessel a minute later,
she would have been completely destroyed.

That skeptic had touched on the weakness of Colt's system
that most disenchanted the military. Underwater explosions
were routine for the British military engineers. The trick was to
set off the mine when the enemy vessel was exactly overhead, a
trick that required a sensitive plotting arrangement, which may
indeed have been that famous secret Colt so ferociously concealed.

Sam's own report said the experiment "took place . . . upon
a ship of 500 tons and under full sail with a moderate breeze
and favorable tide."

Two days later, Sigma again gave the Colt invention a great
endorsement:

May this important invention, now brought to the test
of experiment, and proved to be so eminently successful,
prove the happy means of forever preventing the approach
of an invader to shores thus guarded and rendered impreg-
nable by the force of American science and enterprise; and
may lasting honor and merited reward crown the inventor
of so great a public benefit! Twenty-four hours are
sufficient to completely protect the entrance of any harbor
in the Union, for no foe, unless bereft of reason, will run
into the jaws of so certain and so speedy a destruction.

The military were not so effusive. One review said, "As experiments, these, as many others have been, were very beautiful and striking, but in the practical application of this apparatus to purposes of war, we have no confidence."

Even in death the *Styx* became a serious nuisance, for the wreck lay on the bottom, despite Colt's further efforts to blast it apart on April 20, 1844, and fouled the channel, becoming the nucleus of an annoying sandbar that worried pilots almost till the Civil War.

The most prominent scientists in the study of galvanic electricity, Professor Robert Hare, at the University of Pennsylvania, and Joseph Henry, a pioneer in electromagnetic induction, both reported that touching off distant explosions by galvanic action was nothing new. Colt refused to disclose what his system offered that was new. Congress lost interest and the secret went to the grave with Colt.

For an interval, Colt juggled books, stock issues, partnerships in a doomed effort to profit from the telegraph, the invention of his friend and collaborator Samuel Morse, an invention to which he had contributed considerably.

He set up a company that sent swift boats to intercept inbound vessels from abroad so that his telegraph wires could flash foreign news across Long Island to downtown Manhattan a day before its normal shipboard arrival. The Rothschilds in London, using a crude homing-pigeon system, had made fortunes with a smaller margin of advance notice than Morse's invention gave New York speculators, but the New World commodity and stock manipulators were slow to see the potential profit. Even newspaper publishers objected to paying *fifty cents a week* for a one-day scoop on competitors.

Though the telegraph was a far more revolutionary invention, even for warfare, than his repeating firearms, Colt could not sell it to the public. Unlucky in his contracts and partners, Colt faded out of the telegraph business he had done much to launch.

Seemingly blessed with the hide of a rhinoceros, impervious to fortune's most outrageous slings and arrows, Colt nevertheless showed the strains of his many collapsing dreams by assaulting one Joseph H. Patten, "striking him several times in the face with his fist, blacking one of his eyes, knocking him down, etc." The New York *Sun* for July 28, 1845, speculated that the inventor had lost his iron control because the lawyer had just won a judgment of twelve hundred dollars against Colt to pay back bills at the Astor House.

At the same time, down in Texas, where what luck Colt enjoyed had all been generated, great events were shaping up.

In that turbulent republic, freed from Mexican rule in 1836 partly with the aid of Colt weapons, Plains Indians and Mexican bandits ravaged the frontiers, opposed only by irregular mounted troops—not much more than armed cowboy bands— under short-term enlistment as Texas Rangers. Half the able men in Texas served a short hitch in the Rangers, but a corporal's guard of leaders gave the force continuity. Among them, the most famed was Major John Coffee Hays.

Sometime around the period when Sam Colt was obsessed with his mines, Hays came into possession of a .34-caliber five-shooter Colt, almost certainly Texas Navy surplus. He was immediately struck by its possibilities and armed his entire company with the revolvers.

On patrol west of San Antonio, in the Nueces Canyon, the Rangers met a large force of Comanches, who prepared a leisurely assault—obviously little worried by Ranger firepower.

As usual, the Texans dismounted to fire their long rifles. Then, to the amazement of the Indians, instead of digging in and reloading for a second volley, the Rangers mounted and charged, pistols blazing a murderous string of rapid-fire shots. "Powder-burn them," yelled Major Hays.

Comanches toppled from their horses and the survivors fled, jettisoning bows, lances, and shields. Their chief later complained about the unfairness of fighting Rangers who "have a shot for every finger on the hand."

That particular encounter may well be apocryphal, but something much like it must have happened many times as the Plains Indians suffered their first catastrophic contact with Sam's invention. The arrival of repeating firearms had doomed the horse Indian; his bow and arrow became obsolete overnight.

Other Ranger leaders noted Hays's success, and the Republic of Texas was ready to give Sam's fortunes a boost.

VII

From the day the first slaveholding planters crossed the Appalachians and cleared the forests of the lower Mississippi Valley, they had dreamed of a vast slave empire stretching to the Pacific. The big thinkers among them included the islands of the Caribbean, Central America, Mexico, and the Mexican lands west of Texas: New Mexico, Arizona, and above all, California. The capital most often named for the projected empire was Havana.

At the beginning of the nineteenth century, Aaron Burr ruined his career by dabbling in the scheme. General James Wilkinson, who was a paid spy in the service of His Most Catholic Majesty of Spain while he was also the highest-ranking officer in the American military, betrayed both employers by plotting to steal Mexico from Spain, and the southwestern states and territories from the United States, and from the two robberies to patch together the dreamed-of slave empire. Among the conspirators were many other well-known names of American history, among them Philip Nolan, the wild-horse tamer of Natchez who became famous as Edward Everett Hale's "The Man Without a Country" and who was almost certainly a secret agent of General Wilkinson or the United States or both. The inept westward explorations of Zebulon Pike and his subsequent wanderings in northern Mexico as a prisoner are best explained as the work of a secret agent, as a dupe of Wilkinson, to whom he reported, probably in the innocent belief that he was serving his country.

The actual troops who set about conquering an empire by spreading over an entire continent, however, were not the heavy thinkers, the venal conspirators, the ideologists who tried to justify land-grabbing by emitting clouds of philosophical gas. They were simple farmers and drovers who wanted land, mountain men who wanted beaver skins, miners who wanted gold. They were considerably less simple about self-defense than the military in Washington, however, for they did not quibble about paying exorbitant prices to arm themselves with a Colt five-shooter before venturing into the prairie. ·

Among the most famous of the frontiersmen who hunted game and scouted for such major explorers as John C. Frémont and for wagon trains of westward-bound emigrants was Kit Carson. Possibly because of his diminutive size—he was about five feet four inches tall—he early armed himself certainly with a Colt rifle and probably with Colt pistols also. He informed the famed soldier and explorer Frémont (who, incidentally, at five feet one inch was even tinier than Carson) that a small party armed with repeating rifles could defeat an army with single-shot weapons.

Most historians of the Plains cite the encounter of the Texas

Rangers under Major John Coffee Hays on the Pedernales
River in 1844 as the first use of repeating weapons against the
horse Indians. Carson was there three years earlier.

Carson's biographer Edwin Sabin gives an account of the attack on a wagon train by a mixed party of Kiowas and Comanches 175 miles east of Taos, New Mexico, in 1841.

The Carson men distributed themselves among the
wagons, to await the Indian charge. At daybreak, down
swooped the reds—to be lured on by a feeble round of a
few muskets and pistols. But when they were well inside
point-blank range, the whites delivered the first volley;
nevertheless, still the charge continued, for to the Indian
mind the defenders now had only empty guns.

Abruptly and disastrously the galloping warriors were
made acquainted with an evolution of firearms. The Kit
Carson company, according to Oliver Wiggins, was maintained in the highest state of efficiency; the revolving pistol
had lately been adopted; and springing from cover to the
backs of their animals, the trappers met the Indian charge
with a countercharge, shooting right and left without
reloading. Saddle pads were emptied, the Indians broke
and fled, with that accusation which has become historic:
"White man shoot one time with rifle and six times with
butcher knife!"

. . . More than a hundred Indians were killed, while
the whites lost but one man.

. . . According to Oliver Wiggins, Carson was alert and
his men were alert to secure the most advanced ideas in
offensive and defensive weapons; and so his party in the

fight of 1841 . . . were armed with the new revolving pistols of Sam'l. Colt.

At the same epoch that the plainsmen considered a Colt indispensable, Sam, back east, had virtually abandoned efforts to convince the military of their worth. Except for his successes in the Seminole War, his experience with the military had been a series of discouraging reports by ordnance boards rejecting the repeating weapons as unreliable—even worse, rejecting the principle of a repeating weapon itself as unnecessary in warfare. Just as his repeaters were becoming most successful in the field, Colt had been forced to turn his attentions to the submarine-mine and telegraph fiascoes.

Though Anglo-Saxon settlers were pressing westward the width of the continent, the newly formed Republic of Texas—already settled, organized as a government, and next door to the tempting prize of Mexico—was the natural spearhead of the drive for empire.

On June 20, 1841, an idiotic expedition set out from Texas to seize by force Santa Fe, a city then Mexican. They had been armed with Colt revolvers salvaged from the wreck of the Texas navy schooner *San Jacinto*. But that is the only prudent measure they took in preparing the adventure. Nobody knew the road to their objective, there was no quartermaster or logistic support—not even a map of the region. The quixotic filibusters wandered the desert till surrounded by a Mexican force. When the Texans saw capture was inevitable, they smashed their Colt revolvers on rocks. The Mexicans executed a few invaders, imprisoned the rest. Many lived to fight the Mexicans another day, again armed with Colt revolvers.

Though he had not been President at the time of the Santa Fe fiasco, Sam Houston, when he took office, in December

1841, immediately began planning another filibustering expedition to build an empire at the expense of Mexico. In late 1842 he ordered General Alexander Somervell to mount an invasion. President Houston had disbanded the entire regular Army as an intolerable expense, so he suggested that General Somervell use mounted irregular troops—Texas Rangers, in short. As cavalry commander he recommended Major John Coffee Hays, for Major Hays already enjoyed the reputation he still holds in some quarters as the greatest of all Texas Rangers.

Said President Houston: "You may rely upon the gallant Hays and his companions; and I desire that you should obtain his services and co-operation, and assure him and all the brave and subordinate men in the field, that the hopes of the country and the confidence of the Executive point to them as objects of constant solicitude."

By November 18, 1842, General Somervell had recruited 750 men and had left San Antonio, bound for Laredo. Even the unflappable Major Hays must have been somewhat dismayed by his troops, for among the more-or-less honest adventurers and legitimate Rangers were the dregs of a turbulent frontier.

Arrived before Laredo, the force promptly put the town to sack without pretense of provocation, for there had been no resistance and the town was Texan anyhow. General Somervell sent a detachment of dependable men through the camp to gather the loot. He returned it to the *alcalde* of the village with apologies. Appalled by the general's honesty and discipline, two hundred men deserted.

General Somervell crossed the Rio Grande and seized Guerrero. Again he lost control of his troops, who sacked the town. Disheartened by the quality of his so-called command, the general called off the expedition and ordered the men home. Half the men and five of his captains refused to return to Texas. The decision to go or stay did not exactly separate sheep from goats, for, while Major Hays and the famed Ranger captain Ben McCulloch sided with the general, the equally celebrated Big Foot Wallace and a genius of light cavalry tactics named Samuel H. Walker—the man who later gave his name to the Walker Colt—stayed with the other filibusters.

What the President of the feeble Texas Republic hoped to achieve with the mad expedition against what was then a powerful military nation is hard enough to understand—though Houston later showed that he was not above proposing desperate diversions to take the taxpayer's mind off his fiscal troubles.

What the filibusters who stayed on in Mexico planned to achieve—a band of lightly armed men in a foreign land without a base of supplies or the faintest trace of legitimacy—is impossible to guess. They can be understood only as a bandit rabble.

And that is precisely how the Mexican Army handled them. They were surrounded by a force twice their size at the little mud-hut village of Mier, on the Mexican bank of the Rio Grande (site of the present Falcon Dam). Survivors reported that in the ensuing battle the filibusters suffered only ten casualties, while they killed seven hundred Mexicans—a report that strains credulity, especially since they surrendered meekly enough.

The prisoners suffered hardships in an overland march to Hacienda Salada, near Saltillo. Santa Anna, dictator of Mexico, condemned the whole band, but American and British diplomats intervened and persuaded him to execute only one tenth of the prisoners, the unlucky ones to be chosen by lot. In the famed drawing of beans from a pot—159 white beans and 17 black—a black bean meant death. Fortunately for Texas and Sam Colt, Samuel Walker drew a white bean and lived through a prison term in Mexico City to return to Texas and Ranger service.

Though not so impetuous as Sam Houston, many American leaders were affected by that same lust for Latin real estate—especially those Southerners who nourished that dream of an elusive slave empire. John Tyler, of Virginia, in the waning months of his presidency recommended to Congress that Texas be annexed by the extraordinary procedure of a joint resolution, which could be passed by a simple majority of both houses. Tyler resorted to the parliamentary maneuver because he knew he could not command the two-thirds majority of the Senate required by a treaty. The joint resolution squeaked by, and voting was almost entirely on party lines, indicating the country was not solidly behind the expansionist sentiment.

Signing of the resolution was almost the last official act of President Tyler. As a kind of symbol of the continuity of Texas policy, at the inauguration, on March 4, 1845, of James Polk to succeed her husband, Mrs. Tyler wore on a chain around her neck the gold pen Tyler had used to sign the annexation resolution.

The new President had been nominated as a "dark horse" and little was expected from him even by his own party. To everybody's surprise, Polk turned out to be a forceful leader with a strong will—too strong for some tastes, because he set in motion several acts that could end only in war with Mexico.

During this period a journalist used the phrase "manifest destiny" to justify the spread of American hegemony over the continent. The phrase had a nice ring, and politicians took it up.

Polk's only moderate act toward Mexico was sending John Slidell as a plenipotentiary empowered to purchase all disputed lands, plus New Mexico and California. Mexico turned him down.

Already smarting from such Texan provocations as the Santa Fe and Mier expeditions, the Mexican Government was annoyed by the "annexation" but apparently would not have gone to war about it so long as the gringos stayed on their side of the frontier. But there was the rub. To Mexico, the frontier was the Nueces River. To Texas, it was the Rio Grande, parallel to the Nueces but from 50 to 125 miles deeper in Mexican territory.

General Zachary Taylor was then in command of half the entire American Army—about three thousand men—at Fort Jesup, Louisiana, a post named after the general who had given Colt his first military orders, during the Seminole War. On June 15, 1845, Taylor received orders to move to a point "on or near the Rio Grande."

General Taylor well knew that planting American troops on the Rio Grande was an intolerable provocation to the Mexicans, especially since the moderate and peace-seeking Mexican President, José Joaquín Herrera, had been toppled by a firebrand named General Mariano Paredes. The new President not only claimed the Nueces Strip, between the two rivers, but told Slidell that Mexico owned the land to the Sabine River—which meant all of Texas right to the Louisiana border. General Taylor did not immediately go all the way to the Rio Grande, but stopped near Corpus Christi. He did camp on the south side of the Nueces, however, which technically was as serious a provocation, since he was inside the disputed Nueces Strip, even if only by a few feet.

Before long, General Taylor went all out on the war path by setting up Fort Texas on the bank of the Rio Grande opposite Matamoros. At Fort Paredes, across the way, General Mariano Arista took command of about seven thousand troops, about as many as existed in the entire American armed forces. On the same day, April 24, 1846, he notified General Taylor that so far as he was concerned war had begun. With a fine show of innocence, General Taylor answered that he had committed no hostile act and so "the responsibility must rest with them who commit them."

The American force was not only outnumbered more than two to one, it was an army adapted to a woodland war, suited to conditions on the American Atlantic seaboard. By universal agreement, Mexican cavalry and lancer units were among the world's best. The American Army had no cavalry whatever, but only dragoons, who dismounted to fight as infantry. In the vast spaces of Texas and northern Mexico, General Taylor desperately needed crack horse soldiers as scouts, skirmishers, and couriers. He found them in the Texas Rangers.

Responding to his call for volunteers came three Ranger regiments. One of the regiments arrived afoot, a strange means of conveyance for Texas Rangers. One of the mounted regiments was made up of merchants and farmers of the East Texas farm country.

The third regiment was led by John Hays, by this time a colonel, who, some historians say, had introduced the Comanche nation to the Colt revolver the hard way on the Pedernales. Among its captains were such hard-bitten frontiersmen as Samuel Walker, who had finally returned to Texas after his prison term in Mexico City. Virtually all the Rangers in the third regiment carried at least one Colt; most of them carried a brace of revolvers.

Taylor's main force, at Fort Texas, near present-day Brownsville, was an inconvenient twenty-three miles upstream from his supply base, at Point Isabel, leaving his supply line exposed. Captain Walker camped his company midway.

When his scouts reported Mexican cavalry crossing the river, Captain Walker led seventy-five Rangers to intercept them. His scouts had neglected to mention that the Mexicans numbered fifteen hundred. Walker's company wisely scattered, and rallied at Point Isabel. With a six-Ranger escort, Captain Walker dashed back to Fort Texas to warn General Taylor of the threat to his supply base.

Less fortunate than the Rangers, a scouting force of sixty-three dragoons fell into a Mexican trap. They suffered eleven dead and five wounded. Only Captain W. A. Thornton escaped capture, for he shot his way through the encircling cavalry with his personal brace of Colts. He carried word of the disaster to General Taylor.

The general reported to Washington, "Hostilities may now be considered as commenced."

Leaving the fort under command of Major Jacob Brown, on May 1, 1846, Taylor marched to the relief of Point Isabel. Walker's Rangers shuttled between the commands as virtually the only courier and scout force the general had.

Taylor's force hastily built defense works around the supply base and then wheeled back to lift the siege on Fort Texas. At the head of only twenty-three hundred troops and two hundred vulnerable supply wagons, General Taylor reached a little mound called Palo Alto, where Rangers told him six thousand Mexicans blocked his path. Taylor plodded on.

The collision occurred about 2 P.M. on May 8, 1846. The vaunted Mexican cavalry charged, but the American infantry stood firm, doing terrible execution with fixed bayonets. General Taylor's artillery outranged antiquated Mexican guns and further punished the enemy. General Arista, who had lost about four hundred dead to the Americans' nine, fell back to a strong position in a dry river bed called the Resaca de Guerrero. The Americans followed and settled into a facing ravine called the Resaca de la Palma.

From their naturally fortified positions, the forces again clashed the following afternoon, May 9, 1846. The Mexicans again suffered grievous casualties and fled across the river, scores more drowning. That evening, General Taylor raised the siege and renamed the fort for Major Brown, who had died in its defense. (Brownsville has grown up about the fort.)

On May 11, 1846, President Polk publicly restated the American claim to the Nueces Strip and said, "Mexico has . . . shed American blood upon American soil." Two days later, May 13, 1846, Congress declared war. The House then called for fifty thousand volunteers (the Mexican Army numbered about thirty-two thousand) and appropriated a $10-million war fund. Curiously, although the declaration of war carried overwhelmingly (170–14 in the House, 40–2 in the Senate), the bill to do something about fighting the war ran into stiff opposition from sixty-seven congressmen. A representative from Kentucky, Garrett Davis, said, "It is our own President who began this war."

During the night of May 17–18, 1846, General Arista evacuated Matamoros and fell back on Monterrey, deep in Mexico, 175 miles to the southwest. Taylor crossed the river and seized the town before Arista's dust had settled. His force was now in territory everybody conceded was Mexican, and he had begun an invasion.

Following a route scouted by Rangers, General Taylor marched on Monterrey. Among his officers were names destined to become immortal in another war: U. S. Grant, who deplored the Mexican invasion as unprovoked; George G. Meade, who, with Grant, would defend Gettysburg; Robert E. Lee, who would lose a war there; William Sherman, who would break a nation's will by laying waste its heartland; Albert Sidney Johnston, who would fall at Shiloh and deprive the South of its most brilliant tactician; Beauregard; Longstreet; Bragg; Ewell. The officer who would emerge as the outstanding military hero of the Mexican War was Colonel Jefferson Davis, commanding the Mississippi Rifles. More important to Sam Colt and the evolution of weaponry was Samuel Walker, of the Texas Rangers.

On September 21, 1846, the vanguard of Taylor's army found the road to Monterrey blocked by a brilliantly uniformed force of lancers under a famed officer, Lieutenant Colonel Juan Najera. Like John Hays in his surprise attack on the Comanches, the Rangers failed to dismount, dragoon-style, as expected. They charged the startled lancers, broke through the line of spear points, and worked terrible mischief at close range with their Colt revolvers. The lancers ran; the Rangers dismounted to pick them off with long-range rifle shots. More than one hundred lancers died, including Colonel Najera.

Trying to outflank Monterrey's fortifications, General Taylor sent a force under General William Worth to the far side on the Saltillo road. After brisk fighting spearheaded by Ranger companies, one under Sam Walker, General Worth captured all the forts blocking that entrance to the city but the fortified Bishop's Palace.

Ranger scouts reported a massive force of heavy cavalry, infantry, and lancers coming to the relief of the palace. Colonel Hays concealed his Rangers on one side of the road, Walker's on the other. A body of Louisiana volunteers made themselves temptingly visible and vulnerable as bait. The Mexicans bit and rushed into the trap. Rangers poured rifle and pistol fire into the massed Mexicans. Survivors fled to the palace. A cannon blew down the gates, and the Rangers poured through the opening.

Rangers with their repeating weapons beefed up American firepower in street fighting within the city till the Mexican commander petitioned Taylor for a truce to allow him to evacuate the city before turning it over to the Americans. The city fell on September 25, 1846.

General Taylor negotiated with General Pedro de Ampudia an armistice to last eight weeks. At the same time, the enlistments of most of the Rangers expired and they rode back to Texas. Though he had expressed admiration for the fighting qualities of his Rangers, General Taylor showed undisguised relief when they left his command, for their rowdy ways had often shocked his West Pointian notions of proper military conduct.

Two of those Rangers—Hays and Walker—had so distinguished themselves, however, they were offered commissions in the regular Army as officers in the newly formed Regiment of Mounted Rifles. Walker at first refused.

Back east, Sam Colt had been pestering various colonels organizing regiments of volunteers, asking for an officer's commission or for an order for Colt firearms, or, in at least one letter, for both. Everybody turned him down. Some of the letters of rejection showed a shocking lack of common courtesy, for they were addressed, after all, to an inventor of military hardware with some claim to nationwide fame, regardless of the condition of his treasury. Which was deplorable, for he wrote his friend Levi D. Slamb of the United States Navy, "I have failed in my telegraphic experiments and I am as poor as a churchmouse. . . ."

When Colt read in a newspaper of Walker's refusal, on July 18, 1846, he wrote directly to President Polk:

> Lerning through the medium of the press that a vacancy exists in the new rifle Regiment caused by the non acceptance by Captain Walker of Captaincy I desire to offer myself as a candidate for the commission offered to him & in

doing so I beg leave to state that I am governed with a desire to make myself of service to my country.

Colt's hopes were undoubtedly dashed when Walker reconsidered and accepted the commission, but no blessing was ever better disguised.

Samuel Walker had seen much service in the Seminole War and had certainly heard there of the renowned Colt repeating carbines. Since coming to Texas, he had served several hitches as a Ranger under Colonel Hays, a stout champion of Colt firearms, and was at that famous battle where the Comanches first met the weapons, at least in Texas.

Upon being named recruiting officer and sent east to man the regiment, Walker also determined to arm his new unit with the revolvers he had come to depend on—or with even better repeaters from Colt.

Hays and Walker arrived in Washington together in November 1846, and Walker went on to New York searching for guns. Colt, undismayed by Walker's acceptance of the plum he coveted, wrote the Ranger an undated letter asking his support.

Dear Sir:

I have so often herd you spoaken of by gentlemen from Texas that I feel sufficiently acquainted to trouble you with a few inquires regarding your experience in the use of my repeating Firearms and your opinion as to their adaptation to the Military Service in the War against Mexico —I have heard so much of Colonel Hayse and your exployets with the Arms of my invention that I have long desired to know you personally & get from you a true narrative of the vareous instances where my arms have proved of more than ordinary utility—

Such is the prijudice of old officers in our Armey against

aney invasions upon old & well known implimants of Warfare that as yet I have not been able to introduce my arms
in the servis to an extant that has proved proffitable. But I
am in hopes of getting an action this winter in there favor
if I am not disapointed in the recommendations I may be
able to collect to submit to congress.

The wonder is that Colt showed no more bitterness at the
sloth and stupidity of the brass who persisted in rejecting his
weapons though the rest of the world, and most particularly
those who did the actual shooting, had long since accepted them
as not just the world's best, but a quantum jump ahead of second best.

His letter to Walker continued:

I hope you will favor me with a minute detail of all oc-
casions where you have used & seen my arms used with a
success which could not have been realized with arms of
ordinary construction. Let me know at where a letter will
reach Col. Hase. I wrote to him some time since at Mon-
teray but presume he did not receive my letter—

And like the master salesman he was, Colt closed in for the
kill:

Should Col. Hase take the command of the regiment ordered from Texas & desire them armed with my repeaters
I have but little doubt but that his requisitions would be
complied with at once.

It has also occurred to me that if you think sufficiently
well of my arms to earge the President & Secy of War to
allow your company to be thus armed you can get them
the arms are very much Improved since we first commenced there manufacture & I have no doubt that with the

Samuel P. Colt. Engraved by
. Wright Smith from a photograph
y Matthew Brady. *New York*
ublic Library Collection.

Among the most colorful of the
exas Rangers from the early Colt
a—the period before the Walker
olt—was "Big Foot" William
Vallace, an amiable giant of modest
telligence who was mixed up in
rtually every brawl that made
arly Texas history.

3. One of the early Texas partisans of Colt's firearms was Ben Mc-
Culloch. He was a famous Indian fighter as a Texas Ranger captain.
When the Civil War merely threatened, he jumped the gun by putting on
a resplendent uniform of his own design and rounding up a platoon of
volunteers to take the Alamo for the State of Texas. He was killed in
action at the battle of Pea Ridge, in Arkansas. *N. H. Rose Collection in
the Western History Collections, University of Oklahoma Library.*

4. Elected as a drab party hack, James K. Polk surprised everybody, perhaps even himself, by becoming a vigorous President who prosecuted ruthlessly and successfully a war that was widely condemned, even by many of his countrymen, as a crude land grab. *New York Public Library Collection.*

5. Zachary Taylor fired the opening shots of the Mexican War. Mixed among them were several balls from Colt five-shooters, for his scouts were Texas Rangers. He captured Monterrey with large assistance from the pistol-wielding Rangers and shattered a Mexican army at Buena Vista. The crusty old man refused to pay postage due on the letter notifying him that he had been nominated for President of the United States and returned it to the dead-letter office. Tightfisted or not, he was a good enough soldier so that, almost alone among his peers, he ventured an order for one thousand Walker Colts, the order that revived Colt's dead dream. *New York Public Library Collection.*

6. One of the most puzzling characters in American history, Sam Houston thought of himself as a Cherokee Indian, wore blanket and moccasins to his United States Senate seat, and dreamed of a vast slave empire that would swallow Mexico, but destroyed himself politically by refusing to vote for secession of Texas from the Union. Like all Texans, he was an ardent Colt supporter and fought with little success to get Sam some meaty government contracts. *N. H. Rose Collection in the Western History Collections, University of Oklahoma.*

7. "Three-legged" Willie Williamson (so called because polio had atrophied one leg and he moved about on a crutch) was one of the most redoubtable of the early Texas Ranger captains. He later became a frontier judge. It was Willie who pulled a Colt revolver on an obstreperous lawyer and cited as his legal authority "Colt on Revolvers." *N. H. Rose Collection in the Western History Collections, University of Oklahoma.*

8. George Catlin left the easy life of an educated eastern intellectual to roam the savage lands of the Americas painting, before they disappeared, the folkways of the Indians. He was an enthusiastic convert to Colt fire-arms, demonstrated them on the western plains and in South America, and painted a series of advertising broadsides on commission from Sam Colt. *New York Public Library Collection.*

9. Almost as important to the development of the Colt family of firearms as Sam himself was Samuel Hamilton Walker, a soldier and Texas Ranger who first witnessed the destructiveness of Colt firepower in the Seminole Wars, proved it by wielding a five-shooter against Comanches, and collaborated with Sam in designing the famed Walker Colt, which restored Colt's bankrupt fortunes and established the supremacy of the repeating firearm as a weapon once and for all. He probably received a brace of Walkers before going into battle for the relief of Puebla in the Mexican War, but they did him little good for he fell during a hot skirmish with Mexican lancers. *New York Public Library Collection.*

hints which I may get from you & others having experience
in there use in the field that they can be made the most
complete thing in the world—

Walker wrote on November 30, 1846, a letter Colt himself
could not have improved on for public relations. It included an
account of the supposed first encounter of the Comanches with
the Colt repeater:

Mr. Saml Colt
Sir—
In compliance with your request I take great pleasure in
giving you my opinion of your revolving patent arms.
The pistols which you made for the Texas Navy have
been in use by the Rangers for three years, and I can say
with confidence that it is the only good improvement that I
have seen. The Texans who have learned their value by
practical experience, their confidence in them is un-
bounded, so much so that they are willing to engage four
times their number. In the summer of 1844 Col J C Hays
with 15 men fought about 80 Comanche Indians, boldly
attacking them upon their own ground, killing and wounding about half their number. Up to this time these daring
Indians had always supposed themselves superior to us,
man to man, on horse—at that time they were threatening
a descent upon our Frontier Settlements—the result of this
engagement was such as to intimidate them and enable us
to treat with them. Several other Skirmishes have been
equally satisfactory, and I can safely say that you deserve
a large share of the credit for our success. Without your
Pistols we would not have had the confidence to have un-
dertaken such daring adventures. Was it necessary I could

give you many instances of the most satisfactory results. . . .

In his letter Colt had mentioned the possibility of picking up
"hints which I may get from you & others having experience in
there use in the field. . . ." Walker, who seems to have had a
considerable mechanical bent, did not overlook the invitation.
His letter continued:

> . . . With improvements I think they can be rendered the
> most perfect weapon in the World for light mounted
> troops which is the only efficient troops that can be placed
> upon our extensive Frontier to keep the various warlike
> tribes of Indians & marauding Mexicans in subjection. The
> people throughout Texas are anxious to procure your pis-
> tols & I doubt not you would find sale for a large number
> at this time
>
> > Yours very respy
> > S H Walker Capt Mounted
> > Riflemen U S A

Though the letter maintains a pretense that the pair had not
yet met, they must have already spent considerable time together, for other evidence indicates the "improvements" mentioned were already far advanced in planning.

Sometime between the two letters, Walker and Colt met and
became close friends. They searched together for a Paterson revolver for a model, but discovered that volunteers bound for the
front had cleaned out the market. Even Ehlers had taken the
few weapons left from the bankrupt Paterson Company's stock
to Texas, where he was to sell them with an ease that must have
been disquieting to the man who had killed the goose that laid
the golden eggs he had just run out of.

Together Colt and Walker designed a new revolver destined to become world famous. Walker insisted on a heavier caliber, a weapon that would take fifty spherical lead balls to the pound, which works out to .44 caliber. The revolver would also accept a somewhat heavier, ogival bullet, then an experimental projectile being tested with apparent success in America and Europe. Also, the evolving Walker model would fire six shots, thus becoming the eponymous weapon of all the western six-shooters to come. Walker added a trigger guard to prevent accidents while drawing the gun, and he simplified the lock so that the trigger remained visible even when uncocked.

The barrel was rifled with seven grooves turning to the right at the rate of one turn in three feet and was to be a whopping nine inches long. The grip strap was iron, with black walnut grips.

Walker planned to build so sturdily that the revolver would weigh four pounds nine ounces, two and a half times what a modern revolver weighs. Should a Ranger run out of ammunition, he still held in his hand a formidable war club. And indeed in later years Rangers routinely used their Colt solid-frame Peacemakers as bludgeons to subdue prisoners who did not merit killing.

The pair worked like lightning, for on December 1, 1846, only a few days after their meeting and the very next day after Walker's letter supposedly suggesting for the first time a collaboration on a new design, Colt wrote Walker another letter, offering to furnish one thousand Walker models at less than $25 each, a second one thousand at $17.50, and lots of one thousand afterward for $15. With orders of five thousand or more he proposed getting machinery that would drop the cost to ten dollars, "a trifling advance over the cost of a common pistol."

Then Colt had an uncharacteristic failure of nerve and wrote an almost craven letter to Walker offering to make the pistols for virtually any price.

New York Decr 3d 46

Sir: Since seeing you yesterday I have thought that objections may be raised against the price at which I propose furnishing my Pistols by those gentlemen who are still anxeous to defeat there use in the War with Mexeco and our Frontier Service. If you find this to be the cace, & the President is disposed to incurage the use of my pistols by our light troops & will autherise you to contract for a supply, you shall have them on your own terms and of a patern embracing all the alterations and improvements sirgested by you & I will use the greatest possible dispatch in furnishing a full supply trusting to the representation you may hereafter give of them & the justice of Government to reward me for my labor & invention.

Heading the Ordnance Department was a Lieutenant Colonel George Talcott, a crusty archconservative who had earlier quarreled with Colt about some piddling items in a bill for tinfoil cartridges, and so was hardly a friend in court. But Sam Walker managed an interview on December 7, 1846, with President Polk himself, and when the President, with his unexpected firmness of purpose, leaned on Colonel Talcott, the ordnance chief had no choice but to address an order to Colt and on that same day.

7 Decr 1846

At the instance of Capt Walker, the Secretary of War desires you to furnish one thousand revolving pistols, bore fifty to the pound (round ball) with elongated bullet moulds in addition, at twenty-five dollars each in accordance with your letter to the Captain, the whole to be delivered in three months. Please inform this Office whether or not you will engage to furnish the pistols as above. . . .

G Talcott

Lt Col Ordnance

It is noteworthy that Walker got for Colt his full original estimated price and took no advantage of Colt's momentary collapse of will.

At last! Colt had finally caught the will-o'-the-wisp he had been chasing since he quit selling laughing-gas highs and had become a serious inventor and entrepreneur ten years earlier. He had his big military contract.

The only drawback was he no longer had a factory.

At Whitneyville, Connecticut, not far from New Haven, Eli Whitney, Jr., ran an armory producing beautifully finished Jaeger rifles with methods approaching modern mass-production techniques, for all parts were interchangeable. The very day, December 8, 1846, following the ordnance chief's letter, Colt wrote Whitney:

Be kind enough to inform me if you have machinery adapted to the manufacture of repeating pistols and if so would you like to undertake the manufacture of a few thousand for service immediately.

(Colt could not help dangling the bait of "a few thousand," though he had only a very hard-earned contract for a single thousand.)

Whitney's reply is dated the same day, a depressing fact to modern man, who can expect a letter to take two days to a week to make the same journey one way. The canny gunmaker, who probably was acquainted with Colt's shaky finances and bold bluffs, wrote that he had much government work already on hand and that he would not consider the contract unless he had more specifics. He asked the key question, "Have you an order from Govt for your pistols?"

Sam Colt had started thinking big again, for he wrote Whitney: "I am willing to take off your hands all the machinery Tools &c made expressly for this work when the contract is completed whether it be for one or more thousands."

On New Year's Day 1847 Whitney wrote Colt a courteous letter turning down the contract, but adding, "The offer which you make me I am inclined to think a fair one, were I perfectly at leisure to undertake the job."

Colt was not normally a man who took no for an answer; Colt with a purchase order from the Ordnance Department in his pocket was a bulldozer. He rushed along plans to have his revolvers made in Whitneyville.

First, he needed to make a model. He tried to lay hands on a Paterson No. 5 he could disassemble and rework according to the Walker design. Like Walker, he discovered the city had been cleaned out by Mexico-bound volunteers. The few pieces left in the hands of friends were unobtainable because their owners refused to have them destroyed for whatever purpose. Colt's personal pistol was an unsuitable small-caliber vest-pocket model.

Many legends have grown up about Colt's solution to his problem of seeking a model. The truth is simple and straightforward. An old friend and sometime rival gunsmith, Orison Blunt, years later testified in a patent-infringement trial as he showed the court a Walker Colt, "The first pistol of this model was made by me in my shop for Mr. Colt to exhibit to Captain Walker. . . ."

Walker suggested a few changes in the model, principally redesign of the trigger guard and lengthening and thickening of the already massive grip. They were ready to sign an agreement momentous in Colt's career and in the evolution of firearms:

Memorandum of an agreement made this 4th day of January 1847 between Samuel Colt (inventor of Colt's Patent Repeating Pistols) and Samuel H. Walker, Capt. U. S. Rifles, and acting by authority of and direction of the Secretary of War, for the immediate construction of 1000 or a larger number if hereafter determined by the Secretary of War, of said Colts patent Repeating Pistols, made to correspond with the model recently got up by said Colt and Walker and being as follows, viz,

The barrels to be nine inches long and Rifled made of the best hammered Cast Steel and of a bore suited to carrying round balls, fifty to the pound with strength sufficient to firing an elongated ball weighing Thirty-two to the pound.

The cylinders to be made of hammered cast steel with chambers for six charges each, and of a length, size, and strength, sufficient to be charged with an elongated ball 32 to the pound.

The lockwork with the exception of the hammer to be made of the best cast or double sheet steel and the parts sufficiently uniform to be interchanged, with slight or no refitting.

The Hammer and lockframe to be of the best Gun iron and case hardened.

The stock to be of sound black walnut, bound and secured by a stong strop of iron.

The Pistols answering to the above specification to be

maid with the least possible delay, and to be paid for at
the rate of $25 each on delivery—in New York in passels
or lots of 100 each. The first hundred of said arms to be
completed, if possible, in three months from the date this
contract is confirmed by the Secretary of War, and all the
remainder as soon thereafter as possible, and not under
any circumstances to exceed five or six months if the arms
can possibly be completed by the dividing up of the work
or the employing of two sets of hands to work night and
day.

A noteworthy clause requires parts to be interchangeable.

The agreement also provided for cones, screws, molds, flasks,
screw drivers, nipple wrenches, and levers to service the
weapons.

Walker left for Washington with one copy of the memorandum; Colt tackled Whitney and, by January 13, 1847, had
somehow badgered the gunsmith into undertaking the project.

The New York *Emporium* had repeated with some anxiety a
rumor that an unnamed mechanic with a contract to supply the
Mexican Government with Colt revolvers was about to sail for
Mexico. "We are proud to say he is not an American."

The New York *Morning Express* of January 5, 1847 reported that Captain Walker had gone to Washington the previous day after contracting for one thousand Colt six-shooters for
his new mounted rifle regiment, each man of which was to be
armed with a brace of the repeating pistols and a rifle. "It
was found impossible to obtain any number of these pistols in this city, such has, of late, been the demand for them
from soldiers and others going to Mexico."

The paper could not know, of course, that the pistols Walker
had ordered did not even exist.

The *Express* added that the mechanic of the rumor reported by the *Emporium* was a German who had worked at Paterson and who had left for Mexico with chests of tools and machinery. The mysterious German herewith disappears from notice, probably because he never lived outside of rumor. The anxiety stirred by the unfounded story, however, demonstrates how much higher Colt weapons ranked in the public mind than among the high brass. New York journalists considered the possibility of Americans facing Mexican-made Colts to be a calamity, while Colt was getting petty orders from his own government with all the ease of pulling teeth.

Colt considered the redesigning of the standing breech and cylinder arbor radical enough to merit another patent. He further designed a machine to cut the new parts and leased it to the Whitneyville Arsenal for $1.25 a pistol, the machine to belong to Colt at the completion of the contract. Whitney's shop foreman, on January 18, 1847, signed the agreement and the plant began paying Colt back some of his money for the privilege of using his specially designed tools. It is no wonder that Whitney had had polite misgivings about getting involved in business with the shrewd Yankee inventor.

Whitney subcontracted much of the work. Forging and boring of barrels went to Slate & Brown, of Windsor Locks, Connecticut; William Ball built thread mills for making nipples. Colt held men to their benches for exhausting hours by tripling, even quadrupling, the going rate of a dollar a day. He recruited as many former Paterson men as he could. (As a side observation, discovery among the effects of one of the Paterson mechanics of a Walker pistol that never saw Mexico shows that taking home "samples" of the company's product is not a modern invention.)

Walker kept pestering Colt for a pair of pistols as demonstration models to persuade congressmen of their superiority; Colt could not get through to the Ranger that factories did not turn out products two at a time before proceeding to the next pair. A sample letter from Walker:

> The president and Secretary are, they say, both disposed to give one what I recommend, and refer the matter to Congress, and *they* will not act with out seeing a proper speciman of the arms—but it is useless for me to waste any more time in arguments with a set of asses to convince them of the importance of getting your arms.

Walker had to leave Washington to take up his basic mission, recruiting mounted riflemen. He made his base at Fort McHenry, in Baltimore, the same fort that had given proof through the night to Francis Scott Key that The Star-Spangled Banner was still there.

Sometime during this recruiting duty, Walker sketched a scene of the famous 1844 introduction of the Colt to the Comanches. The inventor turned it over to the engraver O. L. Ormsby, who made a die that impressed the scene on the cylinders of the revolvers. Walker rides a black horse on the left side of the scene, Hays rides a white horse on the right. The stamp became the hallmark of Colt revolvers.

Walker filled out a company and moved them to Newport Barracks, Kentucky, for training. The frenzied note of Walker's first letter to Colt from Kentucky should have been enough to persuade any congressman that the redoubtable Ranger was not joking about wanting to take some Colt revolvers into Mexico.

Newport Barracks Ky
March 19th 1847

Dear Colt

. . . do for heavens Sake rush things as rapidly as pos-

sible and send me some of the Pistolls immediately I want
to commence drilling my men on horseback with them I
have now 120 men with me and will enlist 180 more to
take out with me, everything now is depending on you, let
me hear from you immediately if not sooner and let me
know when they will be forthcoming, find out how things
are likely to work in relation to inspection &c and let me
know all about it. Could you not get Mr Whitney to turn
all his force upon them and turn them out immediately if
you will only manage to get them turned off rapidly and
forward me enough to arm my detachment before leaving,
"you shall wear the brightest Laurel of our first victory
and the Glory shall all be thine," yours in haste

S H Walker

Capt M. R.

Rcetg officer

Colt wrote on March 21, 1847 to Colonel Hays that he
would have enough weapons to arm Walker's company by the
end of April and the rest by the first of June. Then he cannily
pointed out that on completion of that contract he would have
"mashinery & Tools sufficient to enable me to turn out at the
rate of five hundred Pistols & Rifles a month. . . ."

He lamented, however, that "Colonel Talcott and the officers
of the Ordnance Department are deadly opposed to my arms
and the only way to get orders for them is to approach the President first and get him to instruct the Secretary of War."

Colt did not keep his promise to arm Walker's company before they left for Veracruz by steamer. Walker wrote him a letter from there, reading, "I have a fine set of young men that will
give a good account of themselves as soon as they have the opportunity. You must try your d------t to send me those pistols."

That letter incidentally addresses Colt as "Peacemaker," the first time the title was used.

The Walker models may have been lacking, but there were many Paterson Colts on the scene at the siege of Veracruz, for the New York *Morning Express* published a dispatch reporting that five hundred volunteers armed with Colts had planned to run an armed merchant vessel to the fort at night and scale the walls by the vessel's yardarms. (The author of the plan and commander of the force was David Farragut, who only fifteen years later led a Union fleet to the capture of Confederate New Orleans and ultimately the whole Mississippi River and who supposedly said at the battle of Mobile Bay, "Damn the torpedoes, full speed ahead.") The castle surrendered before the boarders could carry out their plan.

The reporter was disappointed. "I wish most heartily they had been permitted to carry it out— It would have been something unique of its kind, and would have shed undying luster on the navy."

The collapse of Mexican defenses at Veracruz on March 27, 1847, and its occupation by General Winfield Scott two days later, incidentally, is as nice a bit of poetic justice as history records: During July of 1846 the exiled former dictator of Mexico, Santa Anna, had dickered with American agents in Cuba to give to the United States for $30 million the Rio Grande as the Texas boundary and great chunks of Mexican territory farther west including Upper California. He agreed to pass military information to the Americans. On August 16, 1846, he was slipped through the American naval blockade and landed at Veracruz.

Intrigue was Santa Anna's very life, and he—a double agent in the service of the United States—soon denounced the treachery of former President Herrera for trying to negotiate a peace with the United States. President Paredes fell from power and his successor named Santa Anna to lead an expeditionary force to clear Taylor out of northern Mexico. Santa Anna himself became President on December 6, 1846. To make his treachery complete, he marched an army of about twenty thousand men northward in February 1847.

General Taylor had violated the spirit of orders from Washington to stay put at Monterrey and had moved westward to Saltillo. His Ranger scouts, led by Ben McCulloch, brought him word of the alarming advance of a vast Mexican force outnumbering the Americans three to one. The forces clashed on February 22, 1847, in a mountain pass three miles north of the Hacienda de Buena Vista. For a time, the Americans were in extreme danger, but Taylor's expert artillerymen rescued him again and a ferocious counterattack by Jefferson Davis's Mississippi Rifles won the day. Santa Anna abandoned the field, his force decimated and soon scattered.

When General Winfield Scott landed at Veracruz in the first major amphibious landings in American history, the Mexican soldiers who might have buttressed the defense to throw him back into the sea were lying dead or wandering without discipline in the far north, where the treacherous Santa Anna had wasted their power.

On April 8, 1847, General Scott, with nine thousand men, left Veracruz for the interior.

Colonel Hays's Mounted Rifles and the unruly Ranger companies acted as a cavalry screen, ran messages, escorted supply trains, scouted, and ran off guerilla bands.

Officers of more conventional units wrote letters home expressing astonishment at their uncouth appearance. Albert Brackett, of the Indiana Volunteers, wrote that the Rangers were

an odd-looking set of fellows, and it seems to be their aim

to dress as outlandishly as possible. Bob-tailed coats and long-tailed blues, low and high-crowned hats, some slouched and others Panama, with a sprinkling of black leather caps . . . and a thorough coating of dust over all . . . their huge beards gave them a savage appearance.

He then noted the essential that set Rangers apart from other troops far more than their bizarre dress:

Each man carried a rifle, a pair of pistols and . . . two of Colt's revolvers; a hundred of them could discharge a thousand shots in two minutes.

Though awed by their firepower, Brackett still underestimated the impact of a Ranger broadside. They could easily fire thirteen hundred shots in perhaps no more than forty-five seconds—a devastating storm of lead. It is no wonder the other soldiers were impressed by the shock power of Ranger armament, for, more than three decades after invention of the percussion cap, most of them went into battle carrying flintlocks.

At Cerro Gordo Pass, on the road to Jalapa, Santa Anna dug in thirteen thousand men behind fortifications to block the road to the capital. American engineering officers scouted a route that outflanked the Mexican earthworks so Americans could take them from the rear. Despite brave fighting, the Mexicans were routed. (Two of the young officers who found the flanking route fought in the same battle for the last time at Antietam, Maryland, seventeen years later; they were Robert E. Lee, who commanded the Confederate invaders, and George McClellan, who commanded the Union troops that stemmed the invasion. Outstanding hero of Cerro Gordo was the W. S. Harney who was Colt's first friend in the Army, the officer who bought the first carbines in the Seminole War and used them to crush the "Spanish Indians.")

The enveloping movement made possible by the reconnaissance trapped 204 Mexican officers, 2,800 men, 43 cannon, and 4,000 small arms. Americans lost 63 killed and 300 wounded.

General Scott reached Puebla, only two hundred miles from Mexico City, on May 15, 1847. Because the clumsy system of short-term enlistments robbed him of one third of his force, he had to hold up there for three months while he rebuilt his army. When General Franklin Pierce (later President of the United States) arrived with three thousand reinforcements, Scott was ready to move on. He left behind, however, a garrison of about twenty-five hundred men, most of them ill or walking wounded.

Back home, Colt was closing out his first contract and wrote the Secretary of War suggesting that an order for five thousand more pistols would make possible a 20 per cent discount off the twenty-five dollar price. He added that his "workmen are well instructed & will leave me unless I have immediate inducements to keep them together— It would be difficult to replace them—"

(Secretary of War W. L. Marcy awarded him another grudging little contract for one thousand more pistols, but it was large enough to cause Colt to gather up the machinery that fell to his lot on completion of the Whitneyville contract and move it, in late 1847, to a factory of his own at 22 Pearl Street, in Hartford, where he remained for most of three years.

General Scott entered the Valley of Mexico on August 11, 1847. Santa Anna had powerful forces, perhaps twenty thousand altogether, concentrated about Contreras and Churubusco. On August 19 and 20, 1847, about three thousand Americans routed the defenders out of strong positions at both points, but at great cost—133 killed, 865 wounded, or about 15 per cent of those involved, far more than the one-tenth casualties normally considered excessive. On the other hand, Santa Anna lost seven thousand soldiers, more than 30 per cent of his force. He fell back on the capital, five miles away, and sued for an armistice.

During this Armistice of Tacubaya, from August 24 to September 7, 1847, diplomats struggled to make a peace, with no success.

General Scott resumed the offensive, and at the battles of Molino del Rey and Chapultepec defeated the Mexicans but suffered heavy casualties. His troops chopped their way through the city walls and occupied Mexico City on September 14, 1847.

The war was not over. The capital city's populace was unruly; even worse were many of his own volunteer troops, foremost among them the Texas Rangers.

At the Zócalo, in the city's center, a Ranger lifted some candy from a peddler's cart and refused to pay. The Mexican unwisely threw a stone. He was riddled. A young boy twitched a handkerchief from a Ranger's pocket. He was shot down. In the red-light district, somebody stabbed to death Ranger Adam Allsens. His comrades seized the district and in a single night of terror laid eighty corpses in the streets.

On September 16, 1847, General Scott issued General Order No. 20, an extraordinary measure that went far beyond the Articles of War in defining military crimes and methods of dealing with soldier criminals. The order organized a local system of justice and is widely regarded as America's first effort at military government of a conquered people. The order was clearly aimed at his own volunteers, including the Rangers.

Santa Anna renounced the presidency and joined the army, under General Joaquín Real, that had laid siege to the enfeebled American garrison at Puebla. General Scott ordered General Joseph Lane to march from Veracruz to the relief of Puebla.

From the Castle of Perote, about halfway between Veracruz and Puebla, Captain Sam Walker fretted, impatiently waiting for his Walker Colts. The shipment did not arrive before he had to march to Puebla, and so there is much confusion about whether Walker ever saw the finished product of his genius. On October 5, 1847, however, he wrote his brother Jonathan, in Washington, a letter that seems to clear up the mystery.

Dear Brother

I write in haste to inform you that I leave here tomorrow under command of General Lane in command of three other companies of Cavalry with the expectation of fighting Gen. Santa Anna at the pass of Pinon about fifty miles from this place. He is said to have a force of eight thousand men. But I must confess that I have some doubts about his meeting us voluntarily our force being upwards of three thousand men. We will move light with as few wagons as possible. . . .

. . . Santa Anna seems determined not to make peace and seems disposed to continue the war under all circumstances. I look upon this determination as one of the most fortunate events that could transpire. As it will leave us the alternative of taking military possession of the country; which will finally result in the Annexation of Mexico and open a new and extensive field for the display of American genius and enterprise.

Sam Walker clearly had no illusions about why he was fighting; he was chasing the old dream of empire and foresaw nothing less than annexation of the entire republic.

His letter continues his eight-month-old yearning after the pistols for his mounted rifles.

> . . . If I had my revolving pistols I should feel strong hopes of capturing him or killing him. I have written three times to the different officers at Vera Cruz to forward them and two commands have come up since they arrived at Vera Cruz but I have no hope of getting them until Jack Hays comes up. I have allso made repeated applications to go for them but without success. . . .

After lengthy paragraphs about family trivia, Sam Walker adds a paragraph that seems to indicate that somebody had troubled to send him the brace of Walker pistols hand-selected by Colt for his personal armament.

> I have just recieved a pair of Colts Pistols which he sent to me as a present, there is not an officer who has seen them but what speaks in the highest terms of them and all of the Cavalry officers are determined to get them if possible. Col. Harney says they are the best arm in the world. They are as effective as the common rifle one hundred yards and superior to a musket even at two hundred yards. . . .
>
>   S. H. Walker

Then Samuel Walker added a startling postscript:

> P.S. I have been one month under arrest by Col. F. H. Wynkoop the cowardly creature who was the first to retreat since the commencement of the war and that from an insignificant force of the enemy.

Apparently, General Lane had a higher regard for Captain Walker's soldierly skills than Colonel Wynkoop, for the postscript adds that Walker had been given command of three other companies—which is at least a major's job.

On his arrival at Perote, General Lane sent Captain Walker and his three companies forward as a vanguard. At Huamantla, Walker, with about 250 men, encountered about 1,600 Mexicans entrenched in the adobe houses of the town.

The action that followed is obscure. Every correspondent had a different version.

It is reasonably clear at least that the gallant Captain Walker led a charge through the streets. His mounted riflemen scattered a force of lancers, picked snipers off rooftops and out of windows, and trampled down opposition till the town had been triumphantly cleared.

When the smoke cleared, his comrades found Sam Walker lying dead in the central plaza. According to some legends, he had been stabbed in the back with a lance wielded by a father seeking vengeance for his fallen lancer son.

In any case, the codeveloper of the Walker Colt was dead. Though his fellows must have lusted after the beautiful brace of Walkers he carried to his death, the pistols were forwarded immediately to his family.

General Lane lifted the siege of Puebla on October 12, 1847.

Santa Anna fled the country, protected by an American *laissez-passer* that enraged the Rangers, who could barely be restrained when his carriage passed.

The Rangers fought other skirmishes against guerillas who infested the countryside, but the war in Mexico was effectively over. On February 2, 1848, by the Treaty of Guadalupe Hidalgo, the Rio Grande became the Texas boundary and Mexico ceded New Mexico and California to the United States. The cession included parts of present Utah, Nevada, Arizona, and Colorado. The troopers of Generals Scott and Taylor had gone a long way toward acquiring the dream empire.

And Sam Colt was just beginning to build his dream empire.

VIII

With his own factory, his own troop of trained mechanics under contract, his own government order for one thousand more Walkers, Colt felt himself arrived. His old agent, Dr. C. B. Zabriski, who had spent the war years as a surgeon with the 1st Illinois Volunteers, wrote Colt inquiring about resuming his duties as a sales representative. Colt answered on December 11, 1847, and permitted himself a bit of gloating:

> I will state to you just how I am situated. I am making arms on my own hook altogether on a borrowed capital. . . .
>
> The government has ordered me to make a second thousand of these arms varying a little from the Walker model which together with a pocket gun which I am getting up for market will occupy me all winter with a force of 40–50

hands which I have now employed. As said before I am working on my own hook and have sole control and management of my business and intend to keep it as long as I live without being subject to the whims of a pack of dam fools and knaves styling themselves a board of directors. . . .

He proposed to Dr. Zabriski that they meet in Washington to talk business.

. . . you could spend the winter in Washington and aid my present agent there . . . and share with him the premiums I give him on sales.

His agent was General John Mason, and Colt conceded that it was the general's influence that had won him a contract for the second thousand Walkers.

. . . with proper management at Washington it will be easy to get an order for 5 to 10,000 for arming our Cavalry in Mexico at present prices ($28 each with accessories).

Colt cited a letter from General Zachary Taylor saying of the Walkers that "under all circumstances they may be relied upon." The general, fresh from the battlefield, thus stated an opinion exactly the opposite of deskbound ordnance officers who repeatedly had rejected the revolvers as being unreliable.

During his entire career, Colt worked ceaselessly at stacking up a dossier of letters of recommendation from military celebrities. With a fine sense of public relations, he lavished gifts of his pistols on those in high places. As he said to Dr. Zabriski of the Taylor letter, "With such recommendations as these I apprehend but little difficulty in Washington of getting big orders. . . ."

To offset enemies in the Ordnance Department, Colt had expended great energy as a lobbyist during his many trips to Washington and he had enlisted many warm and powerful friends, especially among Texans. One of those Texas friends was Thomas J. Rusk, who had been a general before election to the Senate in 1846. He wrote Colt on December 14, 1847, asking him to send a pistol as a demonstrator—"one of good quality."

The dig about "good quality" apparently was somewhat justified, for the weapon Senator Rusk received burst during a demonstration before the military committees of Congress. In a letter to General Mason, Colt unloaded blame for the embarrassing accident on government inspectors and Colonel Talcott.

> . . . the bursting of cylinders . . . may possibly have happened . . . the cause for which may readily be traced to the unreasonable strain put upon them by the Ord Dept in their proof, which is enough to burst a sixpounder—
> The success of my arms in the hands of our troops in Mexico in the face of their condemnation by the fat head of the ordnance bureau must I think have irritated him. . . .

Government inspectors were the bugbears of Colt's life. They subjected his pistols to horrendous tests that Colt said overstressed the cylinders and barrels, causing failures in the field. Even his attempts to improve the mechanism caused delay, for inspectors refused to allow any deviations from contract specifications, regardless of how much they improved performance.

General Mason had been making many private sales to dignitaries in Washington, but Colt could not fill them till the military contract was satisfied. With elephantine sarcasm, in a letter to General Mason, Colt did mention one loophole:

Every Pistol that I have sold which was condemned by the Government inspectors after wasting four months time in humbugery over them at a cost of not less than $4000 to me in furnishing men to waight on, alter & fix to suit there whims in some caces more injureous than beneficial, I have sold for $35 each so you see that it is only necessary to have my arms condemned by the ordnance department to raise there value in the estemation of men who pay there own money for them. . . .

I doubt verry much if I can spare you aney unless the government offissers are *kind* enough to condemn some for me. . . .

Nevertheless, Colt was a serious inventor and had to grant existence of some design flaws. Early in 1848, while still producing the second thousand .44-caliber Walkers, he shortened the cylinders a half inch for a reduced powder charge, cut the prodigious, nine-inch barrel to seven and one-half inches, and made other adjustments, including a curious new rifling that started at one turn in twenty-two inches for the first two thirds of the barrel and increased to one turn in sixteen inches for the last third, giving the bullet a last flip before leaving the gun. (The technique was called a gain twist.)

Colt called the new pistol an Improved Holster Model. The pistol carried many other names during its long career, but today it is known as the Dragoon Number 1 and is one of the most popular and famous hand weapons of all time. After incorporating only minor changes of design, Colt sold two hundred thousand Dragoons before they were supplanted by a later model. Even then, the weapon that replaced it was based on the Dragoon.

Senator Rusk and Colt had become so cozy that the gunmaker began writing or dictating letters for the senator's signature. Increasingly impatient with the piddling orders he had been pulling out of the Ordnance Department, he had Senator Rusk sign a letter sent directly to Secretary of War Marcy urging that the War Department buy five or ten thousand Colt revolvers because

> . . . the suppression of the Guerilla and Robing parties will also do more than could possibly be done to create a good feeling for us with the population of Mexico . . . one hundred men armed with Colts pistols would be more effectual for that purpose than four hundred armed in the ordinary manner.

To the President, on March 2, 1848, Senator Rusk wrote a letter that first dismissed the flaws of some specimen weapons as caused by inexperienced hands and cited again the ten years of outstanding service in Texas. Though the Mexican War had ended, with the Treaty of Guadalupe Hidalgo, exactly a month earlier, the senator from Texas knew only too well that Indian and bandit troubles were just about to begin.

> Believing that the power rests with you to order a full supply of these valuable arms for the defense of our extended frontier *without further legislation* we must respectfully ask that you will at once order them to be made. We do not doubt but that 5000 mounted men armed with two of these pistols and a rifle each would do more service then twenty thousand armed in the ordinary way, thereby saving to the Government hundreds of thousands of dollars

annually and affording protection as well to the parties against Indians as to small parties passing through the Indian country.

President Polk balked at ignoring Congress and suggested presenting to the two chambers a joint resolution authorizing the purchase.

By April 25, 1848, Senator Rusk had introduced his joint resolution to buy five thousand pistols at the same price as the first thousand—though Colt had always urged a large purchase with the argument that he could make pistols considerably cheaper in large lots. The Senate passed the resolution on the second reading. The House delayed. Dr. Zabriski undertook vigorous lobbying, often showing off his marksmanship with the revolver, which appears to have been impressive. Secretary Marcy offered to buy another piddling thousand. Senator Rusk urged Colt to grab the contract.

Feeling that he had more friends in Washington than Rusk realized, Colt refused the order and proceeded with manufacture of five thousand, contract or no.

Returned to Hartford, Colt made a disconcerting discovery. Luther Sargeant, his shop foreman, reported that two key workmen, Joshua Stevens and William Henry Miller, had fallen sharply behind in their quotas. On an unannounced visit to the machine shop, Colt and his foreman surprised the two working on a revolver design of their own. Worse, the design had certain undeniable improvements over the Dragoon. After a stormy scene, the two workmen walked out and took their design to the shop of Edwin Wesson, a single-shot sporting-rifle manufacturer of Hartford. They had apparently been scheming for some time with the Wesson brothers, Edwin, Daniel, and Frank, because on July 18, 1848, the day after the confrontation, Sam whipped off a letter to Senator Rusk charging a conspiracy between the dishonest workmen, the Wessons, and his old enemy Talcott, who seemed destined to go through the ages as head of Ordnance.

I discovered yesterday that two of my principal workmen are engaged with several other persons in getting up a repeating pistol with the hope of avoiding my patents, and that they are in correspondence with the Ordnance Department which encourages them in every way. . . .

Speaking of Talcott, he wrote:

. . . I have invariably been defeated by that man and his associates, and I believe this has also been the fate of every other individual who has submitted anything of merit for his approval where the credit & gain was not bargained away to him.

This last move of his favoring a piracy upon my invention as a last resort, had better be kept to ourselves until I can get all the facts clearly proved & officially sworn to— and at a proper time, should his cloven foot show itself in the congress the information we may have will be made to tell when he least expects it.

Senator Rusk must have added the letter to his dossier on Talcott with some pleasure, for there is evidence the senator was quietly preparing a trap for the ordnance officer.

Rusk sent another letter, on August 15, 1848, to President Polk. He repeated his arguments on the need for repeating weapons on the frontier, cited the failure of the joint resolution to pass the House before adjournment, and reported that at the senator's own urging Colt was proceeding with manufacture of five thousand Dragoons in "the confident opinion that at least five thousand of them would be purchased."

To clinch the argument, Senator Rusk enclosed no fewer than thirty-five letters from the most celebrated officers and frontier fighters, the popular heroes whose admirers could conceivably swing an election. The letters are almost fulsome in their praise of Colt's revolvers.

As a form of moral blackmail, Colt made sure all pertinent officials knew he was making five thousand pistols, while waiting bravely for the government to come to its senses and buy the lot. He so wrote Secretary of War Marcy on August 18, 1848, and added a note that helps clear up the tangled nomenclature of his early Dragoons, a problem that has plagued collectors.

The first thousand Walkers used in Mexico were stamped USMI, for Colonel Hays's United States Mounted Infantry. The second thousand, manufactured in his own Hartford plant, were similarly marked. At some point in their manufacture, he had modified them to the style later called Dragoon, so that some of the earliest Dragoons are marked USMI.

Colt added: "Those I have now in the works (by the suggestion of Col. Harney) I have marked and numbered United States Dragoons." This lot was the third thousand in production since Walker helped redesign the revolver.

So it was the influence of Colonel Harney, who was apparently rearming his 2d Dragoons, that caused Colt's popular weapon to be dubbed the Dragoon.

Though he was entangled in Washington's red tape, Colt's fortunes looked more promising elsewhere. Europe had caught fire; revolution was sweeping the Continent.

As early as January 1848 a revolt against the Bourbon kings in Palermo, Sicily, was temporarily successful and broken only by a merciless bombardment that earned the Bourbon King Ferdinand II the popular nickname of King Bomba. On February 22–24, 1848, the French revolted in Paris, and King Louis

Philippe abdicated, turning the throne over to his grandson, the
Comte de Paris, who in turn was rejected by the people in favor
of a republican provisional government. On March 12, 1848,
demonstrations broke out in Vienna; Prince Metternich resigned. Three days later, revolutionaries proclaimed a new republic in Venice. William II of Holland forestalled rebellion by
ordering reforms of the constitution. In Berlin, King Frederick
William IV had to grant a constitution. For five days, rebels in
Milan rousted out Austrian oppressors and ruled their city. In
April the Poles of Cracow also rebelled against Austrian rule.

Angered by suppression of the Polish revolt, French laborers
overturned the provisional republican government and set up
their own communist government. The Minister of War, Louis
Cavaignac, conqueror of Algeria, in the notorious June Days
massacre killed thousands of Parisian workingmen, and their
government collapsed.

Austria was forced to suppress a Czech revolt in Prague.

On September 24, 1848, the revolutionary Louis Kossuth became head of the Committee for National Defense of Hungary,
in effect the dictator of a provisional Hungarian government independent of Austria. He was hailed as a great patriot in the
United States.

Even in Canada, rebellion against British rule smoldered and
broke out the next year in Montreal, where the October Manifesto proposed annexation by the United States.

In Ireland, already restless from centuries of oppression and
starving from the potato blight, authorities arrested the head of
the Irish Confederation, and Tipperary was aflame. A correspondent to the Baltimore *Sun* wrote:

> Five thousand of Colt's revolvers, with the other etcet-
> eras in the hands of the Irish patriots, would effect more

for the independence of Ireland, than the millions in the shape of money, &c, which have been sent to that country.

That same momentous year, 1848, Karl Marx and Friedrich Engels issued the Communist Manifesto, a doctrine that threw the ruling classes of the Western World into an uproar.

As a manufacturer of firearms, useful to rebel and ruler alike, Colt had followed those tumultuous events with more than passing interest.

On October 6, 1848, a sometime friend and New York promoter named George A. Landers wrote Colt about the possibility of doing some fishing in those troubled waters:

> Mr. Allinda, the agent of the Sardinian Government, is delighted with your pistol and has written to his Govt for instruction to buy two or three thousand. I told him that you would let him have them at thirty dollars, the retail price in New York being thirty-five—he thinks he will get the order but as time is everything, he advises that you send them out on private account and will himself take an interest. I propose that we form a company to advance you twenty 2 dollars on each pistol and that you receive one-fifth on all sums above that for which they may be sold. . . . With the active influence of Alinda I think they can be sold to Sardinian & Sicilian Governments at forty or fifty dollars—you will by this means receive the amount our Government are to pay you and at the same time introduce your pistol into active European service which will be a fortune to you.

Without naming the source of capital, Landers advised "not to hesitate to accept the advance of twenty dollars. It will be to the interest of the parties advancing the money to obtain the highest possible price."

The freewheeling Mr. Landers had not done business with Sam before and apparently did not realize he was dealing with a very cagey customer. The obvious shadiness of the scheme, the shuffling back and forth of money through several hands with attendant opportunities for slipping the occasional dollar out of the pack, would not have bothered Colt, for he had frequently displayed the sensitivity and business ethics of a man-eating shark. But the vagueness of the source of that advance money and the instability of the very Kingdom of Sardinia apparently did not reassure Colt. (Despite the presence of the Italian hero Garibaldi in his army, the King of Sardinia was indeed crushed in battle the following year and forced to abdicate.) Colt did not follow through on Landers' proposal.

On December 21, 1848, the Ordnance Board made another of its drearily predictable reports:

> In special cases such a weapon may be advantageous, but it will be found that this will be the case with individuals, not large bodies . . . these repeating arms are neither suitable nor safe for the Armament of troops.

In the face of enthusiastic endorsement of repeating weapons by field soldiers from the Seminole through the Mexican wars, the Ordnance Board had the gall to write, "This capacity of continuous fire is an advantage which they consider as greatly overrated."

Senator Rusk and the legendary Sam Houston, then a senator from Texas, with a Mr. Pilsbury and a Mr. Douglass, called on Secretary of War Marcy immediately after Christmas. When Mr. Marcy repeated the blitherings of Talcott—now dignified as a brigadier general—Senator Rusk lost his temper. He reported the scene to Colt.

"I told him I was done applying to him about anything, but

that I had the safety of our frontiers at heart and the opinion of all the experienced officers of the Army with me, and that I was not going to stop. There was a Congress and—" Senator Rusk uttered a carefully measured threat—there *"would be another Secretary of War."*

The chastened Secretary Marcy asked for a few days to think things over.

The same day, Senator Houston wrote Colt with only cursory mention of what must have been an unpleasant scene. He had his mind on something else.

"When will you be here? When you do come, if you have a small pistol, or will soon have one made of choice quality, I wish you to bring it with you as I wish to purchase one."

Fully aware of Sam's habit of lobbying by making gifts of his finest weapons, the wily old senator hardly expected to receive a bill for the pistol. He urged on Colt a sure cure for tensions and disappointments: "Get married and lie warmer, Sam!"

Houston had little worry about acquiring one of those .31-caliber pocket revolvers, for Sam sent many as gifts to Ranger captains, military men, and politicians. The pocket pistol became extremely popular as a personal weapon in a day when a gentleman did not feel properly dressed without his pistol. Colt made eleven thousand in barrel lengths from three to six inches.

Despite the frustrations of dealing with General Talcott and the irreducible stupidity of ordnance experts, Sam Colt was becoming immensely prosperous, for throughout the world, private collectors, revolutionary juntas, peace officers, frontiersmen—everybody but his own country's military—was clamoring for his wares.

In far-off California another bonanza, almost as crucial for his fortunes as the Mexican War, was shaping up.

IX

In January 1848 in the Sacramento Valley, California, a mechanic named James Marshall, while building a sawmill for John Augustus Sutter, discovered gold. Because Sutter wanted to continue a simple life as a farmer, word was slow to get out; inevitably the rumor escaped, but was only partly believed. During his annual address to Congress in December 1848, President Polk officially let the very large cat out of the bag and the gold rush of '49 was on.

Virtually every adventurer heading for California, whether around Cape Horn, across the narrow neck of Central America, or overland through the United States, went armed and, if possible, with a Colt Dragoon or pocket pistol.

Competition for the emigrant trade was weak, for the Colt was the overwhelming favorite. Most popular of the non-Colts was the Allen "pepperbox," a preposterous weapon with a revolving cluster of barrels rather than a revolving cylinder. In *Roughing It,* Mark Twain's account of his voyage across the Plains, he gives the classic evaluation of the "pepperbox" as a weapon:

He wore in his belt an old original "Allen" revolver, such as irreverent people called a "pepperbox." Simply drawing the trigger back, the hammer would begin to rise and the barrel to speed the ball. To aim along the turning barrel and hit the thing aimed at was a feat which was probably never done with an "Allen" in the world. But George's was a reliable weapon, nonetheless, because, as one of the stage drivers afterward said, "if she didn't get what she went after, she would fetch something else." And so she did. She went after a deuce of spades nailed against a tree, once, and fetched a mule standing about thirty yards to the left of it. Benis did not want the mule; but the owner came out with a double-barreled shotgun and persuaded him to buy it anyhow. It was a cheerful weapon—the "Allen." Sometimes all of its six barrels would go off at once, and then there was no safe place in all the region roundabout but behind it.

The Dragoon, on the other hand, was scoring triumphs in informal trials of marksmanship at jump-off points for the trek across the Plains. One report cited a *pistolero* who put six shots inside an eight-inch circle at fifty paces, extraordinary shooting by any standard.

Colt expanded his lobbying to include the Plains by sending a pair of revolvers to Brigham Young, leader of the Mormon Church and founder of Salt Lake City. The formidable Mormon troops, organized to protect outlying colonies, bought several hundred Colts. Shrewd Mormon merchants laid in a stock for

sale to emigrants passing through Mormon lands to settle farther west.

Colt's private trade spread even into Mexico, the region that
had best reason for respecting his repeaters. On January 10,
1849, he received a letter from Dave K. Torrey, a merchant adventurer who roamed the backwoods of Central America doing
any kind of business that came to hand. He mentioned a just
completed trip to Mexico with, of all people, Colonel Hays.
They had run out of provisions and "subsisted 25 days on roots
& mules instead of 30 days were out 3 months." Undaunted, he
was already planning a return trip as soon as he could load two
pack mules.

> . . . I made an enquires how much your armes would
> sell I judge ther can be quite a number disposed of and I
> intend to see the Gov of the State of Chihuahua to try to
> have his troops furnished with them to fight Indians. I
> learn that many can be sold at the different ranches at a
> good price.

Torrey added that both Ben McCulloch and Jack Hays had
complained of the burden of the heavy, .44-caliber Dragoons
and asked for lighter pistols to wear on the belt. He enclosed a
firm order for eight pocket pistols with six-inch barrels. That
Torrey was a shrewd merchant emerges from this letter on two
counts: 1. He sold Colt revolvers all over Central America.
2. The pocket model did indeed become preferred by emigrants
because of the enormous weight of the larger-calibered Dragoon.

The new President appointed George Crawford Secretary of
War to replace William Marcy, who had seemed to the Colt
faction suspiciously close to the enemy Talcott in sabotaging
military acceptance of the repeater.

Apparently Senator Rusk had uncovered a definitcly unhealthy link between Marcy and Talcott, for he waited till Marcy had gone before dropping on Crawford's desk what Senator Isaac P. Walker of Wisconsin called in a letter to Colt "a bombshell." The bomb did not go off immediately but ticked away under the arrogant Talcott, who continued to swagger in blissful ignorance of the coming explosion that would blast him out of Colt's path.

Even more important to Colt than removal of the obstructionist Marcy was the hiring, in March of 1849, of Elisha Root, the mechanic who had saved young Colt from a tanning at the Ware Pond underwater explosion fiasco twenty years before. Over the years, he had acquired a reputation as one of the most brilliant factory overseers in New England, a man who had refused an offer of a supervisory post at the prestigious Springfield Armory. Colt hired him away from the powerful Collins Axe Company by simply offering to double his salary, whatever it was. Colt once again demonstrated his ruthlessness in this stealing of a prime hand, for one of the owners of Collins Axe was a cousin, Harris Colt.

It is hard to say what contributed most in succeeding years to development of the mass-production techniques and masterful use of machinery to replace human labor that astonished the world and forever changed the course of American industry. Colt's neighbors in New England, at that period the most technologically advanced area in the United States, early took notice of his industrial genius. Shortly after Root took over as supervisor, a reporter toured the plant and wrote:

> Each part of the pistol passes through an almost endless variety of hands; each one, with his peculiar machine, performing some particular portion of the work, but the most curious and interesting machines are employed in making and forming the multiform and complicated lock frame.

Were we ever so skilled in the use of tools we would not engage to make by hand, during our natural life, one of these frames in the perfection which they are here made in a few minutes by this wonderfully perfect machinery.

Every part and portion of the work is done by machinery and with more than clockwork accuracy.

Those praises seem much ado about nothing today, but the reporter was writing in an age when the gunsmith was the most painstaking of artisans, proud of being able to shape by hand the smallest part of his masterworks. Turning the work of producing parts over to dumb machines and entrusting their assembly to many hands, each performing only a single function, was a stunning revolution.

Only a few days after taking office, Secretary of War Crawford ordered a third thousand Colts intended for Colonel Harney's 2d Dragoons. That is when Colt began stamping the new design with the device that gave them their name. He had, of course, been plugging away at making them anyhow in the serene certainty the government would see the light.

Senator Walker wrote on March 22, 1849:

I have made application in writing to the Secretary of War for an order from the $50,000 appropriation. . . . You have seen the regulations prescribed by Secretary Crawford for emigrants wishing arms, requiring *each* applicant to make affidavit that it is his intention bona fide to go to California &c. Old Talcott has had this put in a Circular Letter & added that Colt's pistols cannot be issued by the Government as they have none, leaving the impression that they never will have any.

Senator Walker wanted to know how soon the first Dragoon order—the third thousand—could be ready and how soon he could get two thousand more. "Col Jack Hays wanted enough pistols to arm 3 or 400 Texans who are going out to California."

The senator, who was selling pistols on the side, asked for a dozen Dragoons. "I could sell them at the trade price with ease and as fast as I sold at trade prices, send you the money & receive more."

Sam replied that he was not rushing on the order for the Dragoons and would not cut his price of twenty-eight dollars to the government when he could get thirty-five dollars from private sales—as Senator Walker's own eager request for pistols to sell in Washington at trade prices indicated. For that reason, Sam Colt was not so deeply thrilled by the emigrant bill as his Washington supporters thought he might be. He had no interest in selling to a grudging government at wholesale prices when he was hard pressed to fill orders at retail prices 40 per cent higher. To Sam, every emigrant armed through the fifty-thousand-dollar appropriation was a lucrative sale lost.

The year 1849 was dominated for Colt by the expiration of his first patents and also the need to expand patent protection for his new designs in Europe. He set his well-oiled machine in motion to take care of the Washington lobbying and sailed in late spring for Europe to look after foreign patent protection.

Testimonials submitted to the Senate supporting his case should have hideously embarrassed the ordnance bureaucrats, who even at that late date were dismissing not only Colt's arms but the principle of repeating arms in general. The testimonials came from the most distinguished and battle-hardened officers in America and furnished a chorus of praise for the inventor and implied rebuke for the desk generals.

Major G. T. Howard, of the Texas Regiment, and Captain Sutton, of the Texas Rangers, jointly reported that since 1839

Colt's repeating pistols had "given the combatant more confidence and greater spirit of defiance in those hand to hand struggles with the prairie Indians, than any other arm now in use."

Paying tribute to a manly foe, the two Texans continued:

Those prairie tribes ride with boldness and wonderful skill, and are, perhaps, unsurpassed, as irregular cavalry. They are so dextrous in the use of the bow, that a single Indian, at full speed, is capable of keeping an arrow constantly in the air, between himself and the enemy, therefore, to encounter such an expert antagonist, with any certainty of doing execution, requires an impetuous charge, skillful horsemanship, and a rapid discharge of shots, such as can only be delivered with Colt's six-shooters.

Captain S. G. French, assistant quartermaster of the Army, citing a year's service on the Texas and Mexican frontiers:

Such confidence was reposed in those pistols, that whenever I had occasion to send small parties in advance, or to employ express-riders to carry the mails through Indian country, it was always made a condition, that they should be furnished with Colt's revolvers; otherwise they would not risk their lives in such service.

Senator William Gwin, of California:

The Indians in the gorges of the Sierra Nevada are terrified into honest habits, by the miners in that region being armed with these pistols.

Captain G. H. Tobin, of the Texas Rangers, addressed himself particularly to the monotonous refrain of the Ordnance Board:

As to the objection raised by persons who had had no

experience in the use of these arms, that they may not stand exposure, I would relate the following fact: Major Ben McCullough with 16 men, returning to Texas, after the capture of Monterey, in an encounter with the Camanche Indians lost one of these pistols, after having discharged three chambers. Three months afterwards, he and I, and some others travelling over the same ground, found the pistol, where it had lain exposed to the storms of the whole season, and putting new caps on the nipples of the two loaded chambers, they were discharged as though they had been loaded the day before.

Colonel George W. Morgan saw clearly the revolutionary quality of repeating pistols as a cavalry weapon. In modern times, he said, infantry had been able to stand up to cavalry because the bayonet was superior to the saber.

In the field of Waterloo we have a case directly in point. The French cavalry charged the English squares, time and again, without effect; and, finally, became so desperate that they sought to back their horses through the English formation. Let us suppose the cavalry to have been armed with Colt's repeaters; that, after having drawn the fire of the squares, they had borne down upon them with the rapidity of thought, poured into their faces six well directed vollies. I will not say that such would have been the result, but there is a strong probability that the squares must have melted away before such a storm of balls.

Among the crowd of officers offering ardent testimony to the proven combat value of Colt repeaters appeared again the trusty Colonel Harney, who cited once more his Everglades experience with repeaters in the Seminole Wars. By his exploits in the Mexican War, Colonel Harney had become so admired a military celebrity that his word carried immense weight.

Amply persuaded by the torrent of favorable mail from the most respected combat veterans, authorities renewed the patent for seven years as of the retroactive date, March 1849.

Overseas, Colt left drawings of his new models at the patent offices of London, Paris, Brussels, Berlin, and Vienna. His applications encountered no difficulties.

On some obscure business for Landers, Colt traveled to Constantinople for an audience with Sultan Abdul Mejid I. The sultan was somewhat of a freak in Ottoman history, for he was a kindly, progressive, and even honest man. Throughout his life he struggled with a bureaucracy as cruel and corrupt as any in history. He tried to provide equal justice and religious freedom for all social classes. He labored for universal education. He tried to suppress the slave trade. When the Hungarian patriot Kossuth fled Austrian vengeance after the collapse of his Hungarian rebellion in 1849, the sultan gave him refuge and refused to turn him over to the Austrians.

Most important to Colt and Landers, he was reorganizing and revitalizing his armed forces.

How much business Colt did for the Hartford plant nobody knows. He presented to the sultan a brace of superbly decorated Dragoons and received jeweled snuffboxes and a gorgeous medal encrusted with stones that bestowed some degree of Turkish nobility long since faded out of memory. (Newspapers in the United States wrote indignant editorials when Customs required Colt to pay duty on his gifts from the sultan.)

Colt did some interesting business in long arms, however, and the transaction hints at hanky-panky in high places.

The promoter, Landers, wrote Colt that he had bought one hundred thousand unused muskets from the U. S. Army at the end of the Mexican War. He offered Colt 7 per cent commission on the first fifty thousand sales at five dollars each, 10 per cent on further sales. Those muskets, complete with bayonet and still packed twenty to a case, had cost the government twelve dollars. Because the United States had only a fraction of one hundred thousand men under arms in the war, the preposterous size of that order and the haste in selling them at 42 per cent of their value immediately after their manufacture indicates almost certain corruption. The officer ultimately concerned in such a shady transaction and most likely to profit from a rake-off had to be General Talcott, head of the Ordnance Department, Colt's old enemy.

For a fast dollar, Colt could let bygones be bygones, and so he sold some of the muskets to several of the rebellious bands around the Mediterranean who shed much blood in the name of patriotism and freedom but achieved little beyond changing despots.

Returned home, Colt found that the estimable Elisha Root and his other company officers had been looking after his interests. Root had taken it upon himself to retain attorney Edward Dickerson, of Trenton, New Jersey, to pursue the matter of possible infringement on the Colt patents by the Wessons and the errant mechanics.

They had also put the California trade on a business basis. From the beginning of the gold rush, peddlers had carried across the Plains as many Colts as they could afford, for travelers returning eastward reported a Colt brought as much as two hundred dollars in gold dust in the turbulent mining regions. Once exposed to the rowdy climate of boom towns, prospectors arriving from the East, already armed with Colts, were reluctant to part with them for any price.

Merchants as aggressive as the Colt organization could

scarcely allow a market so lucrative to be served by such hap-
hazard deliveries. It was his able and faithful company officers
who seem to have organized the first regular service, for it was
in January 1850, just after Colt's long absence in Europe, that
Captain F. W. Macondray, of San Francisco, advertised for sale
the first regular shipment of Colts, mostly three-inch and four-
inch pocket models, with a few heavy Dragoons.

Development of the Colt business was stimulated by a curious army policy. General Persifer Smith, sent to California soon
after the peace treaty with Mexico to take over the Pacific Department, not only permitted but encouraged his officers to
moonlight in commerce. William Tecumseh Sherman, then a
lieutenant, wrote, "As there was very little to do, General Smith
encouraged us to go into any business that would enable us to
make money."

The regiment of one of the volunteer colonels who had
rudely rejected Colt's application for a commission at the beginning of the Mexican War took the general so literally that they
deserted to the last man and fled to the gold fields.

The chief commissary for the Pacific Department, Major
Amos B. Eaton, was married to Elizabeth Selden, cousin of the
Colts of Hartford. Major Eaton wrote Elisha Colt, Sam's cousin
and treasurer of the Colt company, inquiring about setting up
an export business to California. From January 24, 1851, till he
dissolved the arrangement, in 1854, he sold seventy-six thousand dollars worth of pistols.

The factory had sold more than ten thousand of the pocket
models alone. Frederick Law Olmstead wrote of a trip through
Texas in 1850, "There are probably in Texas about as many revolvers as male adults."

The Hartford papers gave prominence to any dispatch from
the Far West praising the local product. From Fort Laramie,

Wyoming Territory, the *Daily Times* reported that their correspondent had wounded a buffalo bull with a rifle shot, causing the bull to charge. He reloaded the rifle on the run and hit the bull again. Still no results. He threw down the rifle and fled with fading hope, for the bull was gaining, when he remembered his Colt.

> When I drew the revolver I had little faith in its power to save, having frequently heard that a bull buffalo skull would resist a rifle ball fired even at a short distance.

He put one pistol shot into the buffalo's head and dropped it cold.

Though the factory was booming to fill the emigrant demand and Colt got his patent extension, he feared he would not profit from it. A combination of Wessons plus the two mechanics he had fired, Stevens and Miller, and a clutch of other manufacturers and financiers formed the Massachusetts Arms Company to produce revolvers according to the design Colt had rejected in firing his workmen. So long as Talcott was at the head of Ordnance, Colt stood last in line for government orders. Colt had Dickerson file a suit for infringement of his patents.

Colt found that back home his peddling of munitions to revolutionaries had by no means hurt his standing. Still close to their own revolution, Americans were almost solidly behind the insurgents abroad. The Taylor administration even instructed a special envoy, A. Dudley Mann, to assure the Hungarian revolutionaries of Kossuth that the United States was prepared to grant recognition to their independent government immediately, should they succeed in splitting away from the Austrian Empire. The Austrians were naturally outraged and instructed their Washington chargé d'affaires, Chevalier Hulsemann, to file a strong protest.

Before the Austrian envoy could act, on July 4, 1850, President Taylor, after laying the cornerstone of the Washington Monument, cooled himself with a draft of tainted milk, and died five days afterward of something like typhoid fever. Millard Fillmore succeeded to the presidency and named the great orator and defender of the Union Daniel Webster as Secretary of State. It was Webster who made a historical declaration in answer to Chevalier Hulsemann.

Though he had opposed annexation of Texas, the Mexican War, and other expansionist adventures, Webster defended the right of the United States to take interest in foreign revolutions, because those "events appeared to have their origin in those great ideas of responsible and popular governments on which the American constitutions themselves are founded."

Webster could not deny himself the cocky taunt of a newly born great nation just beginning to flex its muscles: "The power of this republic, at the present moment, is spread over a region, one of the richest and most fertile on the globe, and of an extent in comparison with which the possessions of the House of Hapsburg are but a patch on the earth's surface."

To increase his standing with the military establishment overseas, including the revolutionary camps—and for his own vanity—Sam had always lusted after a military title. He backed Thomas Seymour in the race for governor of Connecticut; Seymour won, and on November 30, 1850, named Colt his aide-de-camp, a position that automatically conferred the rank of lieutenant colonel and the honorific "colonel." For the rest of his life, Sam clung to the long-coveted title.

X

Over the winter of 1850–51, the factory moved into larger quarters, on Grove Street in Hartford.

Because even such staunch defenders of the Colt system as Ben McCulloch and Jack Hays complained of the unwieldy size and weight of the Dragoon, Colt designed another pistol halfway between the .31-caliber pocket models and the .44-caliber saddle-holster weapon. The new pistol took the same-size ball—.36 caliber—as the Paterson pistols that had made his reputation in Texas before the Mexican War. As a salute to those pioneers in the use of revolvers, Colt engraved what he called "the new Ranger size pistol" with a scene from the victory of the Texas fleet over the Mexican Navy on May 16, 1843. Possibly because of the engraving, or more likely because one of the first orders for the new model came from the U. S. Navy, the pistol became known as the Navy Colt.

It weighed only two pounds ten ounces as against the Dragoon's four pounds one ounce, and that weight approaches the norm for modern revolvers. Even more than the immensely successful Dragoon, the Navy became the base of Colt's worldwide fame. More than two hundred thousand of the 1851 models left the factory. Another forty thousand New Model Navy revolvers and thirty-eight thousand Navy models assembled in London made it one of the most widely used handguns of the century. When it was redesigned after Colt's death and beefed up to .45 caliber, the beautifully balanced weapon was named the Peacemaker and is widely credited with having subjugated the wildest elements of the West and buttressed law and order. By 1947 almost a million pistols owed their basic design to the 1851-model Navy.

In May 1851 Colt crossed the Atlantic again to London for the Great Exhibition in the Crystal Palace. Though the show was meant to exhibit Great Britain's technological prowess, industrialists of other nations were invited to exhibit. The Crystal Palace itself, the design of a self-educated gardener named Paxton, was in effect only a gigantic greenhouse, but its use of iron and glass interchangeable parts and its graceful and glittering form seized the world's imagination. Though it was meant to stand only for the fair, the public was reluctant to let it go; after the exposition closed, the palace was dismantled, rebuilt at another site, and lasted till World War II, when it was demolished to prevent its use by enemy bombers as a shining landmark on moonlit nights.

A small-time American competitor exhibited some pepperbox repeaters. The overwhelming hit of the show, however, was the Colt exhibit. More than five hundred engraved and polished arms, including a few experimental rifles, drew crowds from the general public. Sportsmen and military men, potential buyers, could count on the colonel for a spot of brandy to oil the purse hinges.

While the boss was out of town, his attorney, Dickerson, seized the chance to pursue the infringement trial against Massachusetts Arms with no danger of a damaging outburst in the courtroom from the irascible Colt. The trial began on June 30, 1851.

The Massachusetts defense rested on proving the existence of revolvers before the 1836 patent granted to Colt. They called in several gunsmiths to so testify and produced a revolver they said had been made before 1836. Dickerson noticed that some parts had rusted more than others, indicating a strong possibility the gun, or at least parts of it, had been artificially aged. After tripping up a few witnesses on that point, Dickerson treated the jury to some ponderous sarcasm: ". . . if the other side intend to infringe Mr. Colt's lever patent . . . they may put their lever in pickle early so that the rust may have time to change before the trial comes on."

The sarcasm told; the jury found for Colt. During Sam's absence in Europe, Dickerson settled with Massachusetts Arms for fifteen thousand dollars in damages. Sam was at first outraged at the small settlement, but he later gave Dickerson a handsome small pistol engraved with the figure of Justice and a large pistol engraved with Sam's portrait. (A later case against the mechanics failed, perhaps because Dickerson did not try it. The court assessed Colt $116.48 to pay court costs of the defendants.)

In Belgium, just across the Strait of Dover from his London office, Colt was suffering more infringement problems. His English representative, William E. Newton, on a trip to Liège in September 1851 idly strolled through the gunshops downtown and found several forgeries of the Dragoon and pocket models.

He engaged a gunsmith, M. Devos-Sera, to watch over Colt's interests in Belgium. The Belgian reported he had caught a glimpse of the trail of a "Jean" Ehlers in some of the Belgian forgeries being sent to Mexico. Colt himself thought Ehlers might have been involved behind the scenes in formation of the Massachusetts Arms Company. By that date, Mr. Ehlers might have been reflecting ruefully that the booming arms factory in Hartford would have been still in Paterson, New Jersey, and under his aegis had he not gone after a fast dollar in 1841.

In England Colt was doing fine. He shipped 450 revolvers in October 1851 to arm British officers fighting the Kaffir War, in South Africa.

Far more important for Sam's self-esteem, Charles Manby, secretary of the Institute of Civil Engineers, one of the most prestigious technical bodies in the world, invited him to speak at their meeting on November 25, 1851.

It was not his revolvers, but his machinery and mass-production methods, that had captivated the engineers. His speech was called "On the Application of Machinery to the Manufacture of Revolving-Breech Firearms."

The core of his speech is in one paragraph:

The manufacture of arms, both in Great Britain and on the continent, is carried on almost entirely by manual labor, the various parts being forged, filed and ground into the requisite form, by workmen at their house, the barrels alone being forged, bored and ground in manufactures established for the purpose, and machinery being employed only for cutting out the stocks. At the Government small arms manufactury at Enfield, under the intelligent direction of Mr. Lovell, steps onwards have, however, been made, in the use of machinery for some portions of the work. Still no general uniformity among the parts can

Lone Wolf, a great Kiowa war
ef, is shown here armed with a
st impressive tomahawk. In the
d, however, he knew well the
ue of repeating firearms and
ost exterminated a Texas Ranger
ol in a famous ambush at Lost
lley. *Soule Collection in the
estern History Collections,
iversity of Oklahoma Library.*

Satanta, the great Kiowa chief,
parently shared with contempo-
y white officers a distrust of
wfangled weapons, for in this
ture, taken long after revolvers
re commonplace among the
es, he still carries his trusty bow.
committed suicide after his
ture. *Soule Collection in the
estern History Collections,
iversity of Oklahoma Library.*

COLT'S REPEATING PISTOLS,

With the latest Improvements of 1844 & 1845.

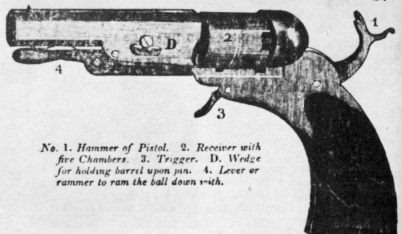

No. 1. Hammer of Pistol. 2. Receiver with five Chambers. 3. Trigger. D. Wedge for holding barrel upon pin. 4. Lever or rammer to ram the ball down with.

The Pistols have 5, Carbine and Shot Guns 6, and Rifles 8 chambers. Pocket Pistols with 2 inch to 3¼ inch barrel, Belt pistol 2¼ inch to 6 inches, and holster or Ship pistol 5 to 12 inch barrel. The pocket pistol will carry from 40 to 50 yards, belt pistol 50 to 60, and the holster or ship pistol 80 to 100, with a very small quantity of powder; and the pocket pistol with ball and cap only, without any powder, from 12 to 15 yards point blank; pistols in Mahogany cases, from $16, $20, $30, to $100.

The above is a true representation of the COLT'S PATENT REPEATING PISTOL; which is acknowledged to be superior in every respect to any other Pistol manufactured in this country or Europe. The Emperor of Russia, the Emperor of Austria, the King of Prussia, the Prince de Joinville of France, the Imaum of Muscat, all have them, and speak in the highest terms of them. The Texan Army and Navy are supplied with them, and the U. S. Navy has been supplied with them to some extent, and the officers have given a most favorable report of Colt's repeating fire-arms. *Great impositions have lately been practised upon the Public by representing and selling the Six Barrel or Self Cocking Pistol as Colt's Patent Pistol.* The Colt's Repeating Pistols, Carbines, and Shot Guns are sold for Cash at reduced prices, at

No. 2 Barclay-street, Astor-house, New-York, by

JOHN EHLERS, *Proprietor.*

W. H. HORSTMANN & Co., *Maiden-lane.*
HYDE & GOODRICHE, *Chartres-street, New-Orleans.*
H. E. BALDWIN & Co.,   "   "
B. DAFFIN, *Ba timore.*
MULFORD & WENDELL, *Broadway, Albany.*

---

12. The first production Colt revolver had no trigger guard, and the trigger appeared only when the hammer was cocked. It also lacked a ramming lever to force the oversized ball into the chamber, insuring a tight seal, so that the very first models were awkward to reload. This advertisement shows that the ramming lever has been added. This lot of pistols offered for sale did Sam Colt no good, for they were among the stock seized by John Ehlers after the Paterson Patent Arms Company's failure. *New York Public Library Collection.*

13. The Walker Colt, designed in collaboration with Sam Walker, packed an enormous wallop. Its .44-caliber ball was pushed by such a tremendous charge of black powder that cylinders and barrels often burst. It weighed twice as much as modern pistols. Between its weight and the kick of the powder charge, strong men were soon fatigued from firing it. But its rapid rate of fire, high accuracy, and long range shattered Mexican cavalry units that tried to stand up to it. *New York Public Library Collection.*

14. Many frontiersmen complained that the Army models were cumbersome to carry, so Sam produced several models of smaller-caliber and lighter belt or pocket pistols, among them the Wells Fargo .31-caliber. *New York Public Library Collection.*

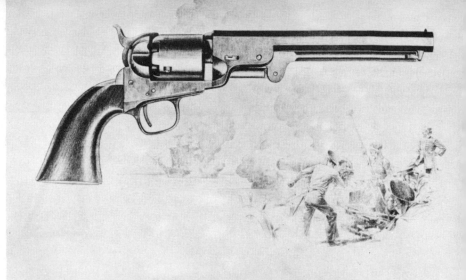

15. Though the smaller-caliber Navy Model (.36-caliber) did not have the tremendous shocking and penetrating power of the .44-caliber Dragoon, its balance and handiness made it the favorite in the gold fields and boom towns of California. *New York Public Library Picture Collection.*

16. The most famous revolver of all time—the Peacemaker. Though it was designed after Sam's death, it descended in pure pedigree from his models. So enthusiastically was it received in Texas that the notorious killer John Wesley Hardin, when he saw a pursuing lawman armed with a Peacemaker on a train in Alabama, cried, "Texas, by God," and tried to draw his own short-barreled Colt .45. *New York Public Library Picture Collection.*

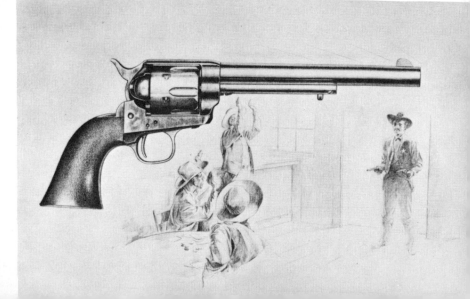

Giuseppe Garibaldi spent a time fighting tyrants, first in the [Ital]ian Peninsula (there was no [lan]d known as Italy in his youth and [for] most of his life), later in South [Am]erica, and again back home. His long battle for liberty fired the [im]agination of the American [peo]ple, so much so that the notori[ous]ly cagey Sam Colt even con[trib]uted a large lot of weapons to [the] cause. *New York Public Library [Pic]ture Collection.*

18. " 'Twarn't God made men equal," goes an old frontier saying, " 'twas Colonel Colt." In this illustration two western ladies, providentially armed with revolvers, are more than a match for a masked bandit holding up the coach en-route from Denver City to Colorado Springs. Stagecoach companies in their handbills routinely advised prospective customers to carry a Colt. *New York Public Library Picture Collection.*

20. A newspaper artist attempted a portrait of John Colt during his stay in the Tombs Prison death cell awaiting execution for murder. It is too late now to learn what happened the day scheduled for his hanging, but it is quite possible the body found on his cot, a knife thrust into its breast, was a cadaver planted by his foxy brother, Sam, after John's escape. *New York Public Library Picture Collection.*

19. An engraving of the Colt Armory at Hartford, Connecticut, showing the onion cupola surmounted by a ball and prancing horse. The armory was the most advanced industrial establishment in America, the largest armory in the world, and almost certainly the most humane mass employer of the Industrial Revolution. *Colt Patent Fire Arms Mfg. Co., Hartford, Connecticut.*

. Caroline Henshaw and the child e indiscreetly named Samuel Colt, ., although the public pretense was at the baby was the offspring of r common-law marriage to Sam's other John.

22. An original Matthew Brady photograph of Colonel Samuel Colt.
N. H. Rose Collection in the Western History Collections, University of Oklahoma Library.

exist, and in America, where manual labor is both scarce and expensive, it was imperative to devise means for producing these arms with the greatest rapidity and economy, and at the same time with such uniform precision, as could only result from the use of self-acting tools.

While he had that prestigious audience captive, Colt could not resist getting in a few cracks at the double-action principle, then most prominently used in the English-made Adams revolver. The inventor, Robert Adams, understandably incensed, claimed the floor and angrily offered one of his pistols for inspection. The embarrassed assemblage persuaded Mr. Adams to sit down and be quiet.

Mr. Manby, who had invited Colt to speak, was impressed enough to join Colt's staff and undertake a search for buildings to house a London branch of the Hartford factory.

On December 9, 1851, Hartford made the first shipment of parts to London for assembly and finishing there, though Colt had not yet found housing for his enterprise.

But the ultimate triumph of what was probably the greatest year in Colt's life was the explosion of Senator Rusk's bombshell under General Talcott.

At Senator Rusk's suggestion, Secretary of War Charles Conrad looked into the nation's reserve stock of cannon balls, though the nation was at peace, with little prospect of war, and a shortage would not have been a grave threat to the nation's security. What he found was heaps, mounds, pyramids, racks, warehouses of cannon balls, stacks of cannon balls in every spare space of every army and navy yard on the Atlantic seaboard. The astonished Secretary observed that orders for still more cannon balls arrived daily.

When questioned, General Talcott said he was merely carrying out the orders of the former Secretary of War.

Secretary Conrad ordered him to cease and desist loading down his peace-loving nation with any more cannon balls. When another order for cannon balls came across his desk, buried in a stack of other papers for his signature, Secretary Conrad knew very well that neither the former Secretary nor he had ordered that particular batch, yet the requisition carried Talcott's signature.

A court-martial followed. It turned out that General Talcott owned an iron foundry in Richmond heavily engaged in the manufacture of cannon balls.

Probably through action of the Old Boys Club, the general's "punishment" was a mere reduction in rank to colonel, removal from office, and appointment as commanding officer of the arsenal in Augusta, Georgia.

The old hypocrite who had preached economy in resisting Colt's superb firearms while decorating every arsenal with immense piles of useless cannon balls of his own secret manufacture had the staggering, almost admirable *chutzpah* to write Colt:

I should suppose you might find time to write to an old friend & one who has shown himself so Zealous & I may say without vanity I believe, efficient in your service.

Back in Hartford, Colt's agents had sold to Juan Manuel de Rosas, dictator of Argentina, five hundred Dragoons with the outmoded square trigger guard Talcott had forced Colt to retain. The volatile politics of Argentina displaced the dictator before Colt could make delivery, leaving the factory stuck with obsolescent arms. On March 10, 1852, Colt wrote Commodore Matthew C. Perry suggesting that he snap up the square-guard stock to outfit the expedition then mounting for the opening of trade with Japan. Another agent had already sold the commodore one hundred Navy pistols through regular channels.

The unpredictable Colt shrugged off the missed opportunity and sent Perry a superb array of decorated and encased pistols to give at his discretion to Japanese dignitaries.

True to his instinct for publicity, on March 30, 1852, Sam wrote from Hartford to his gunsmith-agent in London, Charles Frederick Dennett, of his eagerness to close with the British Government a lease on some Thames-side workshops where he could set up a London factory:

> . . . the most valuable time is being lost & no such hoorah for Colts Arms can again be raised without grate efforts. You must keep the thing as much before the publick as possible. have some of the arms at different shooting galleries & publick places & occasionally get a short spicey notice in the papers of some extreordinary performance by someone of Her Majestes officers with one of them. . . .

And sure enough, within a few days the Calcutta *Englishman* carried an editorial suggesting that Colonel Colt should be told that the first man to mount the ladder at the storming of the Great Pagoda in Rangoon was a barracks engineer armed with a brace of his revolvers.

Colt outlined to Dennett his plan for the English operation:

> I shall take out with me a foreman of the Armoury & some 8 or 10 first rate journeymen or what in England in the shops are caled Enginears.

With a fine note of concern for the well-being of his men he wrote:

> I will want for them a first rate boarding house near the wirkshop where they can live resonable & as well as they can in this country. You know about how such men live

here & they will expect to live as well in England or they may become dissatisfide.

And he added a happy note:

The demand for arms here is unabating & I am dubling up my facilities to make them. . . .

On top of the world, Colt blew off some more of his ebullient spirits in a letter from Hartford on May 18, 1852, to Manby in London:

I am running my wirks with over 400 men a quarter of a day extry time to keep up with the market. If I am able to du half such a business in England as here I will be satisfied yet I du not see why I may not expect it for the good people of this wirld are very far from being satisfide with each other & my arms are the best peesmakers.

Colt's open gloating about the brushfire wars raging or threatening everywhere in the world might not enhance his image for modern historians, but at least they were not the hypocritical pretense of politicians who talked of peace and prepared holocausts for their own and neighboring people.

Besides, Colt's firearms served in other arenas besides the battlefield. In late 1852, E. K. Kane sent in a Colt rifle for repair. The accompanying letter said the rifle had once belonged to Mormons on the Great Salt Lake and had already accompanied him once to the polar sea. He offered to swap the veteran rifle for a new model:

I am preparing for a second expedition in search for Sir John Franklin and am desirous of adding to my list of firearms otherwise I would unconditionally present you with the piece.

The expedition he referred to was one of a series of rescue

missions to find a highly vaunted English effort to traverse the icebound Northwest Passage across the top of North America, an expedition as poorly organized as any in history.

Provisioners had carried aboard the British Navy vessels *Erebus* and *Terror* a three-year supply of victuals, porcelain china, crystal glass, and silver table settings, a 1200-volume library, and a barrel organ with fifty selections. But they carried only a ten-day supply of coal for the auxiliary steam engines, and the 130 officers and men wore only regulation blue uniforms and took no cold-weather gear. They sailed in May 1845 for a land and climate as cruel as any on this planet with the innocence of highborn English babies. Off Greenland, whalers saw the two ships poke into Lancaster Sound, the eastern mouth of the Northwest Passage. They were never seen again.

For the next decade the desolate wastes of the Arctic teemed with expeditions searching for the lost Franklin party.

Among those searchers was the Dr. Kane, a ship's surgeon, who had sent in his rifle for repair or swap. He had been with the first Grinnell Expedition, in 1850, and was at the time of his letter preparing to lead the second Grinnell Expedition.

Should I visit the Polar Regions as is very probably to be the case next Spring your arms will be of service to me. The bears of that region are very tenacious of life and require the repeating arm.

On the second expedition, Dr. Kane carried a Colt rifle to 80°1' north, the northernmost journey recorded to that date.

By reconstructing evidence from caches, skeletons, aerial photographs, and Eskimo legends of astonishing accuracy, historians have determined that the inept English explorers had abandoned their ships, wandered southward across the ice, and starved to death in a region that has supported a healthy Eskimo population for thousands of years. Ten years of search by rescue expeditions, however, did explore and map in record time vast stretches of the unknown Arctic.

Colt's lease on the Thames factory buildings came through, and by June 1852, workmen were cleaning out the empty shops and moving in machinery.

Colt was in a lather to get the English operation going, for Dennett was pressing him hard for guns to sell to private citizens, especially visiting rajahs from India, who eagerly bought any pistols Dennett roughly inlaid with gold floral patterns. By October 2, 1852, sixty cases of machines for manufacture of Navy .36-calibers and pocket .31-calibers and fifteen skilled workmen left aboard the steamer *Pacific* for Liverpool.

England may have been regarded at that time as the world's leader in technology, but Colt had a low opinion. On November 17, 1852, he wrote his lawyer, Dickerson:

> If it want for the cople Dozen Yankey Boys and Yankey Tooles I think I might dispare of ever accomplishing anything. . . . I have to send to Amerreca for such things as a Monkey Rench, a pare of Scales, Blowers for smiths shops. . . . Yet they say here when the Lion wags his tale all Europe trembles now it is my humble opinion that he may wag and be damed so far as mecanick arts are conserned his biggest flerish would not scare the youngest of the Yankey Boyes I brought here with me. . . .

Despite difficulties in getting English production under way—machines began turning only in January 1853—Colt could close 1852 with the satisfaction of having made fifty-five thousand pistols in the Hartford plant.

Business obsessed Colt, but he did take some small care of the responsibilities he had scattered in his wake: Caroline Henshaw Colt Colt, for instance, and Junior, renamed Samuel Caldwell Colt. One authority reports her working as secretary to the governor of Michigan but offers no evidence. Since the same authority repeatedly refers to her as being illiterate—again without offering evidence—the Michigan interlude as secretary is dubious.

Caroline certainly reappears in Bonn, Germany, renamed Miss Julia Leicester and called a niece of Colonel Colt. On March 17, 1853, Colt wrote from London to his new agent, J. Southill, in Brussels:

> I send my "neffue" to Brussels yesterday and directed him to call at your house when he got there and report himself to Miss Julia, Mrs. Southill or yourself. Sammy's book education has been very much neglected to secure him physical strength. He now requires much care for a while to secure for him a thorough education. I have written to Mr. [name left blank] instruction regarding him and Miss Julia. . . . He must have a day or two of play before going to school. Should it not be convenient for you to have him at your own house, Miss Julia will find him a place to stay until he is sent to school.

The oafish use of quotation marks to enclose *neffue* would seem to indicate that Colt wanted to maintain a flimsy pretense that the boy was brother John's son while at the same time letting the world know the handsome lad sprang from his own manly loins. This more or less tacit confession of the boy's parentage only deepens the mystery of what Sam was up to in marrying Caroline (or Julia, as she was renamed) to John in his death cell twelve years earlier. Just as puzzling is Caroline's docile acceptance of his curious maneuvers.

That June, of 1853, Russia occupied the Turkish vassal states of Walachia and Moldavia. The enfeebled Ottoman Empire did not dare go to war alone, so the sultan set about lining up powerful allies only too eager to shed some blood in the endless chess game of European power politics. England, France, Sardinia, and somewhat independently Austria began moving toward war, though nobody, least of all the people who would have to do the fighting, quite understood what the quarrel was all about.

During the years when he was trying to peddle pistols to anybody who would listen and cough up the price, Sam had depended somewhat upon his brother James, a dabbler in politics who was briefly the secretary of the President of the Texas Republic. James moved to St. Louis, fought a famous duel there that embarrassed his family, and won a seat on the bench. For years he had been cadging money from Sam, even at times when the inventor brother was strapped by horrendous debts. James had overplayed the political game, driving himself into deep debt, and asked Sam to rescue him with a job. On August 23, 1853, Sam wrote him from New York:

> What I want you to do in England is to take the entire charge of my business there. You will have to make all purchases and contracts, sign my name to checks in my absence. In fact to have the same position there as Luther Sargeant has in Hartford. For which I pay him $2,500 a year. For your services in London I will give you one half of the net profits of my establishment there and guarantee that the half shall not be less than $4,000 a year.

Naturally, James accepted the position, and with all seemly haste.

Colt needed somebody like James to handle the nuts and bolts of the London business, for matters on the Continent, especially in Belgium, had become vexatious. Arms makers there, licensed to manufacture Colts but not export them to countries where Colt held patents, ignored the contract.

An American importer wrote on December 20, 1852, from New York to the Hartford factory, reporting that he had been offered Belgian Colts at twelve dollars each. Colt answered from London.

> . . . your polite note to me has afforded me the oppertunaty to . . . save you the hazard of contracting for an inferior arm . . . & there importation in the States would lead to legal if not personal difficulties between us—my American Patent has stood the test of our corts & I meen at all hazards & resonable expence to protect it.

Within Belgium, the new representative, J. Southill, was a bulldog. He wrote from Brussels on September 15, 1853:

> I succeeded in the last week in seizing among different workmen and manufacturers seventy three pistols, a work of no small difficulty. They will all be confiscated, and I have brought actions against two for damages, the only ones able to pay. With the others my object is to put down the traffic.

He added ruefully that the imitation Colts were of good workmanship, "very respectable and creditable to the makers. . . ."

Southill reported catching a counterfeiter twice and forcing him to pay fines. On the third offense, however, the offending gunsmith ominously pointed out that he had discovered flaws in Colt's patents, for Colt had not begun production within the time prescribed by law. An alarmed Southill told Colt the man had a point and that Colt should close the loopholes instantly or every pirate in Europe would flock to Belgium to take advantage of the patent failure.

Enclosing for Colt's inspection a small pistol he had found in a shop window, he asked its return so he could use it as evidence. "The man who sold it will wish he had never seen it."

Southill also mailed Colt a prospectus for a school for young Samuel. He also offered to take in Miss Leicester. "Mrs. Southill would be very glad to do a mother's part." He suggested a tutor for Miss Leicester rather than a school, probably because of her age, which would have been somewhere around thirty-one—but a tutor for what? He does not say. Perhaps she was illiterate, as one biographer reports, though there is evidence she spoke several languages and even that one biographer says John Colt taught her to read and write before he died in his prison cell—or whatever happened to him.

Returned to Hartford, Colt was thinking really big. Through dummy buyers, he began rounding up property in a swamp called South Meadows, on the banks of the Connecticut River. Because it flooded each spring, the property had low value till word got out that the industrialist was buying.

According to legend, when Colonel Solomon Porter refused to sell except for an exorbitant price, Colonel Colt established a whorehouse across the street from the holdout to pressure him into selling. Colonel Porter was made of stern stuff, and never sold.

Another legend has it that a Hartford bank demanded an outrageous price, so Colt quietly bought up every note issued by the bank, stuffed them into a bag, walked into the president's office, and told him to sell his lots for a reasonable price or get out—for Colt now owned the bank.

In any case, in the fall of 1853, workmen began enclosing 170 acres of bogland behind a levee to keep out the spring high waters.

XI

With Talcott out of the way, the Grove Street plant humming, and a vast new plant going up on the banks of the Connecticut, Colt had little to worry him about his domestic business.

He reported that the medium-weight Navy pistol for both belt and saddle holster "is now the favorite throughout America for every branch of our service, owing to its lightness and compactness, and it will throw a ball with about the same force and distance as the largest size. And it certainly will do all the execution upon man and beast ever required among buffaloes and American Indians at any distance a soldier can see to shoot any pistol with accuracy."

Overseas, however, the Belgians were still getting under his skin. From London he wrote to Brussels on February 5, 1854, in outrage that the government had not invited Colt to participate in a trial of arms.

A wide contrast does this decision exhibit with that of the French authorities when my arms were to be experimented with I not only had an official invitation with specimens of my arms for trial to be present but the Emperor himself invited me to his palace at St. Cloud to practice with me in a social way the shooting of my arms. He himself shooting one of the specimens about 100 rounds and his generals and aides continuing the practice for allmost the entir day.

As Colt had earlier observed, the people of the world were "very far from being satisfide with each other," and his arms began to appear everywhere a quarrel broke out.

From the Caucasus came a romantic tale accepted as solemn truth by the British press. In April 1854 the *Literary Museum* published one version of the romance that persisted in various forms for years.

COLT IN THE CAUCASUS

In Daghestan, a young Lesghian chief being severely wounded during one of the frequent razzias of the Russians, took refuge in a ruined salki, in order to apply bandages to his wounds. While thus employed, he was discovered by a party of twelve dismounted dragoons, who immediately gave chase, on his taking flight. Being fleet of foot, for a short while he outran them, during which time, such of them as had their carbines loaded, fired at him ineffectually. Having crossed one of the flexible bridges, common in that country, and which was over a rapid torrent at the foot of a mountain, the fugitive, finding himself unable to proceed much farther, and having time to put his arms in order, stood at bay under a projecting rock.

With yells of delight, and uplifted sabers, the Russians

approached the bridge. The foremost, nearing him, cried, "Yield, dog!"

"Not whilst I have twelve lives at my girdle," cried the undaunted mountaineer.

The Russians in the rear laughed loudly at the boast; but he in advance fell dead, pierced through and through by a bullet, nearly at the feet of the Lesghian. The second soldier stumbled over his dead comrade, and as he rose, received a shot which caused him to fall, severely wounded. The next, seeing the same weapon which had twice been discharged, still pointed, rushed on; but, to the surprise of the Russians, a third shot was fired at him; untouched, however, he was about to cut down the Lesghian, when a fourth discharge scattered his brains on the rocky parapet, and his lifeless body tumbled into the torrent.

The story continued with another charge by the baffled Russians which cost them two more comrades. His one revolver empty, the Lesghian drew another from his sash and, because he was about to faint from loss of blood, snapped off three shots at the remaining Russians, though they had retreated to about fifty yards' range. He hit one of the Russians in the shoulder.

"Let us fly," they cried. "It is the Evil Spirit of the mountains." From a distance they looked back. The Lesghian had fainted and fallen behind a rock. "He hath vanished in the mist," the Russians cried.

The report said the pistols were a pair of Colt's revolvers, the gift of an American captain who had visited the wild, mountainous district near the Caspian Sea where the Muslim Lesghians refused to give in to Russian sovereignty for another fifty years. The correspondent also said that since the episode in the

Caucasus many Russian officers had acquired Colt revolvers, so the surprise value was lost.

The story parallels the Kit Carson and Jack Hays accounts of the first use of repeaters on the Plains Indians, and something very much like the duel between the lone Lesghian and the Cossack horde may well have happened.

A Portsmouth, England, paper reported that one thousand Colt revolvers had been dispatched to arm Chinese insurgents and another batch to Borneo. The paper admitted being puzzled over the use of Colt revolvers in Borneo "unless it be promiscuous manslaughter among the natives." The paper regretted that the thousand pistols destined for China had not been kept for the British Baltic Fleet, but added, "What smashing there will be among the teapots and mandarins!"

In March 1854 France and England declared war on Russia, siding with Turkey in a dispute over two minor landlocked satrapies of minuscule, if any, importance to the two maritime powers. Almost the same day, the British Government ordered four thousand Navy revolvers for the Navy. The Army ordered tests to determine if they wanted to place an order.

Unlike the hostile ordnance officers of Colt's own country, the English officers were generous. Though one of the pistols accidentally discharged in the holster and wounded a noncommissioned officer, the board blamed the holster design.

It is our opinion, upon the whole, that Colonel Colt's revolving pistols are good, effective, substantial, and serviceable arms, and with moderate care and attention would answer all the exigencies of service.

Eventually, the British Army bought another eight thousand, to add to the many personal weapons bought by officers. The British press was not happy.

The *Journal,* of Clare, Ireland, published a complaint that was echoed in other papers:

> . . . it seems to have remained . . . for one of our cousins from t'other side of the Atlantic to invent a weapon, which though little more than a pistol in size, produces effects not unworthy of the longer engines of war. Many of the officers in the Army of the Caucusus [Russian] are in the habit of practicing with them, the soldiers, amazed at its extraordinary length of range,— equalling that of a rifle—as well as its repeating properties —have dubbed this admirable arm the Pistol God. There cannot be a doubt as to its vast superiority as a weapon of warfare, and it is a circumstance to be deplored if our military authorities hesitate to fully equip the forces we are sending, both the East and the Baltic, with the weapon in question.

The paper noted the initial order for four thousand Navy revolvers but pointed out that the Baltic Fleet alone could use six thousand. With ironclad logic, the Irish editor argued that so large an order implied faith of the authorities in the weapon's efficiency, but so small an order fell short of what the service needed to wage war.

A Liverpool paper expressed relief that the Czar did not get to Colt first or he "would have 200,000 or 300,000 in the field." Actually, as the Irish paper noted, many of the Czar's officers carried a brace of Colts as their personal side arms.

Colt returned home because the seven-year extension granted as of 1849 was running out and a clique in Congress was trying to cut off further extensions by mounting an investigation into what they said was unbridled corruption and bribery at the time of the first extension hearing.

On July 10, 1854, an ad hoc committee was named to "Inquire whether money has been offered to members or other illegal or improper means used to induce members to aid in securing the passage or defeat of a bill to extend Colt's patent for seven years."

Colt's enemies said that he had engaged a famed lobbyist named Alexander Hays, who maintained an ever-flowing fountain of whiskey in a luxurious hotel suite and offered the services of six girls—three of whom he frankly called "chicks" and three of whom he gave the extraordinary title of "spiritualists."

Colt took the stand and said that since he had not been bodily present at the time the only way he could know of any hanky-panky behind the scenes was through his attorney, Dickerson—but of course that would be hearsay and hence inadmissible as evidence. Mr. Dickerson, on the other hand, was bound by the confidential relationship of client and attorney not to divulge what he had told his client. Colt and Dickerson between them had invented a beautiful Catch-22 to prevent their giving any damaging testimony.

Not all of Congress was happy with the investigation, anyhow, for some suspected that the instigators of the inquiry were themselves receiving favors from rival gun manufacturers. Representative Michael Walsh, of New York, shook up the committee when he proposed an amendment to find if "money or other valuable consideration" had been paid "with a view to causing an investigation of the patent extension granted to Colonel Samuel Colt."

The inquiry fell apart, and an effort to revive it on the floor of Congress was literally hooted down with whistles and catcalls.

In September 1855, action in the war against Russia concentrated on the shores of the Black Sea, where the Allies landed and laid siege to Sebastopol, the Crimean naval base of the Russian Black Sea Fleet. The fighting was dreary, the soldiers diseased and mud-soaked, the British high command dominated by aristocratic boneheads.

Colt's revolvers were there. The steward of a British gunboat reported an adventure with his personal weapon when he went ashore with his purser near Balaklava to buy fresh meat and was attacked by five Cossacks.

In our flight I was struck in the thigh by a spear hurled at us by a cossack. The purser got captured, but soon released himself by disposing of three of them whilst I settled a fourth with our revolvers. The other one, I need not say, made himself scarce in an incredibly short space of time. The Russians call our revolvers infernal machines which have been given to their enemy by the devil, and imagine that they will go off whenever required by invoking his aid; hence the great terror always evinced whenever those weapons are brought forth.

The steward said a spear wound is not painful—like a hot iron on the side entering and a cold iron on the side leaving. Land soldiers were amused by his encounter, he said, because they felt sailors ashore fought on a "harum scarum principle, running here, there and everywhere—killing anybody and everybody who comes in his way."

Not every British officer was enamored of the Colt. Some were willing to exchange Colt's admitted greater accuracy and range for the hitting power of the double-action Adams, which ranged up to a tremendous .50 caliber in size. Lieutenant Colonel G. V. Fosbery recounts an anecdote from the Sepoy Rebellion, a revolt of native troops in India:

> An officer who especially prided himself on his pistol shooting was attacked by a stalwart mutineer armed with a heavy sword. The officer, unfortunately for himself, carried a Colt's Navy pistol, which, as you may remember was of small caliber, and fired a sharp-pointed bullet of sixty to the pound and a heavy charge of powder, its range being 600 yards, as I have frequently proved. This he proceeded to empty into the Sepoy as he advanced, but, having done so, he waited just one second too long to see the effect of his shooting, and was cloven to the teeth by his antagonist who then dropped down and died beside him. My informant who witnessed the affair, told me that five out of the six bullets had struck the Sepoy close together in the chest, and had all passed through him and out his back.

The careful historian notes that these improbable adventures always are reported at second hand, never by an eyewitness. If the incident truly happened, it was a very sturdy Sepoy indeed; several surgeons consulted about the physical possibility of such a clutch on life scoffed at the tale.

Nevertheless, Sam Colt had a serious rival in the Adams. At short range it hit hard and had an even higher rate of fire than a Colt.

A more serious rival appeared when Rollin White, in 1855, patented a pistol cylinder with chambers drilled clean through, making possible the use of metal cartridges. According to legend, he offered the license to Colt first and took it to Smith & Wesson only after Sam refused. If true, Sam's actions locked his armory into the obsolescent cap-and-ball principle till well past his death. It was his good luck that the Smith & Wesson company built only small-caliber models for years before going after military contracts.

British Government orders fell off and Sam wrote a discouraged letter about the English operation:

> We have about 5,000 pistols navy size finished and about 4,500 in the making. I shall not commence anymore here until I have something definite from the government and it is about an even chance if I do not suspend the business of making my arms here altogether and trust to the Hartford establishment to supply the demand this side of the water.

Clearly disappointed in the profit-sharing contract he had made with his brother, James Colt saw the cause in his brother's perfidy rather than a falling off of business. He returned to St. Louis, from where he wrote Sam on July 20, 1855:

> There can be no doubt, I think, in the minds of any honorable men, but that I have been trifled with—trifled with in a manner, the most cruelly wicked of any instance on record.

James, quoting from the balance sheet, noted a twenty-one-thousand-pound profit that was almost wiped out by an unexplained nineteen-thousand-pound deduction.

> The English Armory has made a great deal of money and . . . there is not much doubt that I am entitled to one half of the profits in conformity with the proposition you made me before I resigned my judgeship two years since. If you will not have a settlement with me of our pecuniary affairs upon just and equitable grounds all I have to say is

that I am obliged to go back to my profession after wasting two years without a library and without means to support my family for three months to come. . . .

Colt answered on September 15, 1855, with mysterious allusions to a one-hundred-thousand-dollar loss suffered in Europe, "to say nothing of the notoriety of the matter if the greatest possible care is not taken to prevent my name getting into the newspapers."

Sam offered his brother a position in Hartford.

. . . when I get all my works removed into the South Meadow under my charter organization every prominent man and head of a department will own an interest in the capital stock and should you come here to be at the head of the establishment during my absence I should secure to you an interest in the concern that would bring you in a handsome income if the business is profitable and I see no reason why it is not likely to be so. . . . If you will come here to settle permanently the interest which I give you in the concern I can guarantee will bring you in 4 or $5,000 a year and I think a great deal more but I will not pledge myself beyond 4 or $5,000.

James wrote a sulky letter on September 28, 1855, accepting on condition he received a deed to a cottage on Weatherfield Road and four thousand dollars a year.

The financial calamity Colt referred to was possibly the seizure by a European government of a shipment of pistols Colt tried to smuggle across the country. In his correspondence with London during this period, Colt made many guarded and mysterious references to some kind of customs troubles, perhaps in Belgium. Several years later, the King of Prussia seized a shipment, confiscated and sold the weapons at auction, and levied a stiff fine. The ninety- to one-hundred-thousand-dollar loss referred to by Sam in his letter to James could be converted into English currency remarkably close to the nineteen-thousand-pound deduction James had questioned in the balance sheet.

About that time, the great English novelist Charles Dickens visited the London plant and wrote an article for *Household Words*. In an early paragraph, Dickens undertakes to explain a Colt revolver to his readers and makes a dazzling demonstration of the ability of a great writer to make complex matters lucid though they be quite alien to his normal interests:

> For those who have not seen a genuine Colt's Revolver, we will endeavor to describe some of the advantages of this weapon. The revolving cylinder, behind the fixed barrel, is drilled with six holes, into which, one after the other, the powder is rapidly dropped without being measured; for it is impossible to put in too much powder, if room enough be left for the ball. Six balls are then taken in the hand, and also placed, one after the other, in the holes. These balls are of conical shape . . . and are made of soft lead. They are rather larger than the holes; but a ramrod fixed on a hinge under the barrel, being brought down by a handle, on the lever principle, forces all the balls, in rapid succession, into the holes. The charge being now perfectly air-tight, requires no wadding. At the back of this cylinder, are six nipples, for percussion caps, carefully separated from each other; and the marksman, taking a few caps in his hand; puts one on each of these nipples, upon which the six-shooter is loaded. The caps being at the back, and not at the top of the cylinder, will not fall off in carrying; and, both charges and caps being watertight,

experiments have proved that they will fire after some hours immersion in water. The top of the hammer itself, in a line with a little spike on the end of the barrel, gives the sight for aiming. On pulling back the hammer with the thumb, after firing, the cylinder revolves one-sixth of its circumference, instantly bringing another hole, with its charge, in a line with the barrel. The barrel being rifled, and the charges in the breech, air-tight, none of the force of the powder is lost; and the balls are carried further, and with far greater precision than from an ordinary musket.

Dickens cited several anecdotes about use of the Colt around the world, including that Lesghian chief of the Caucasus who was beginning to become a well-known celebrity in England. With dripping sarcasm, Dickens shot a bolt into the Establishment, which was his lifelong enemy:

> Our own officers at the Cape of Good Hope [fighting the Kaffir War], who were graciously permitted to purchase Colt's Revolvers for their own uses with their own money, relate their marvelous achievements, till her Majesty's Board of Ordnance begin to hear of them.

The writer then leads his readers on a stroll through the shop to marvel at Colt's methods of mass manufacture by use of steam-powered machinery:

> Under the roof of this low, brick-built, barrack-looking building, we are told that we may see what cannot be seen under one roof elsewhere in all England, the complete manufacture of a pistol, from dirty pieces of timber and rough bars of cast steel, till it is fit for the gunsmith's case. To see the same thing in Birmingham and in other places

where firearms are made almost entirely by hand labour, we should have to walk about a whole day, visiting many shops carrying on distinct branches of the manufacture. . . .

"We are independent people," says my informant, "and are indebted to no one, save the engine and fixed machine makers."

This little pistol which is just put into my hand will pick into more than two hundred parts, every one of which parts is made by a machine. A little skill is required in polishing the wood, in making cases, and in guiding the machines; but mere strength of muscle, which is so valuable in new societies, would find no market here—for the steam engine—indefatigably toiling in the hot, suffocating smell of rank oil, down in the little stone chamber below—performs nine-tenths of all the work that is done here. Neat, delicate-handed, little girls do the work that brawny smiths still do in other gunshops. Most of them have been sempstresses and dressmakers, unused to factory work, but have been induced to conquer some little prejudice against it, by the attraction of better pay than they could hope to get by needlework.

Even the men have, with scarcely an exception, been hitherto ignorant of gunmaking. No recruiting sergeant ever brought a more miscellaneous group into the barrackyard, to be drilled more rapidly to the same duty, than these two hundred hands have been. Carpenters, cabinetmakers, ex-policemen, butchers, cabmen, hatters, gasfitters, porters, or, at least, one representative from each of those trades, are steadily drilling and boring at lathes all day in upper rooms.

On the second floor Dickens studied "a long vista of machinery" with girls overseeing the boring and rifling of barrels, "having nothing to do but to watch the lathe narrowly, and drop a little oil upon the borer with a feather now and then."

The writer was entranced by machines that cut steel and wood with equal ease into eccentric shapes. He enlarged on the interchangeability of parts in the Colt system:

> Seventy-odd out of a hundred of the injured revolvers picked up on the battlefield during the Mexican War were repaired with bits of other pistols on the spot.

On the top floor he found workmen without spectacles buffing parts on emery wheels. In a passage that would horrify a modern safety engineer, he recounts the routine use of magnets or "scraping the eyes with the sharpest knife that can be found" to remove splinters of steel.

A single steam engine in the basement drove all the machinery:

> Everybody gets a slice of this thirty horse-power; and my conductor says, they have still plenty of power to spare, as if steam power were an article like gas or water, to be laid on whenever it is wanted from a distant reservoir.

That same fall, of 1855, Sam moved into the South Meadows factory and put into effect the full product of his industrial genius.

Among Colt's innovations was his pay scale. Division of labor inevitably meant that some jobs required more skill than others. The less skilled tended machines and made smaller wages than the artisans, who finished and assembled the pistols. Only 10 per cent of the cost of a pistol went to handwork, another 10 per cent went to machine labor, the rest went for materials, overhead, and the cost of machines. Most wages were calculated by piecework, so that the productive laborer made more money. Colt paid the highest wages in the arms industry and still produced at a competitive price.

Colt published a rule for his workmen:

> Every man employed in or about my armoury whether by piecewirk or by days wirk is expected to wirk ten hours during the runing of the engine & no one who dose not chearfully concent to du this need expect to be employed by me.

In far-off Crimea, the British launched their suicidal Charge of the Light Brigade, the few survivors fell back and the high brass tried to figure out what went wrong—which historians are still doing. Meanwhile, the French launched a conventional attack at Malakhov, one of the fortresses guarding the Bay of Sebastopol, and toppled the defenses with tactically sound methods that inspired no heroic poetry by Alfred Lord Tennyson but did end the Crimean War.

Colt's associate L. P. Sargeant wrote him a letter from London reporting the fall of Sebastopol and correctly crediting the French allies with the victory. The letter also brought news that the American Ordnance Department had no monopoly on fatuous meddling:

> . . . the new management of Ordnance they are more stupid than ever. . . . The most absurd thing which is turned off of late is an order from Lord Hardinge that all the pistols have a hole bored in the handle to pass a cord through so that the arm can be suspended from the neck and after firing the six charges it is dropped and the sabre

taken in hand. Just imagine a pistol dangling and knocking
about while the soldier is slashing with his sabre. I asked
Capt. Dixon what the holster was carried for if not to deposit the arm when not in use adding that his lordship's
plan was most decidedly [illegible].

Sargeant refused to bore holes in his precious pistols and told
Ordnance that after they received them "they could mar them
any way they chose."

Avid for items useful in his perpetual public-relations campaign, Colt seized on the report that the French had turned the
tide of war, and wrote Sargeant, "I am searching the papers to
see new incidents at the Crimea of the gallant use of my repeaters by the French, as well as the English soldiers there."

Among other items he turned up in his search for what he
called "spicey stories" was a report in the Hartford *Daily Times*
that the captain of the *Sovereign of the Seas* had been surprised
by a mutiny while the ship's muskets were stored and unloaded.
A passenger handed him a Colt. He wounded the third mate
and threatened to blow out the brains of the ringleader. With
the revolver, he rounded up eight mutineers and put them in
irons.

On March 26, 1856, the great powers signed the Treaty of
Paris ending the Crimean War.

The people of the world—especially those right in North
America—still were not satisfied with each other, in Colt's
phrase, and the demand for his weapons stayed high.

XII

By that spring, of 1856, Colt had good reason to preen himself. Only nine years before, he had been a bankrupt desperately trying to maintain a façade of prosperity after the successive failures of his arms factory, his submarine-mine scheme, his marine-telegraph company, and the notoriety of his brother's suicide or whatever in a death cell. But by that glorious spring of 1856 he could, with truth, call himself the most prosperous industrialist in New England.

On the South Meadow river flats below Hartford stood an immense brownstone armory, by far the largest private armory in the world. Over it, as a landmark to river traffic, rose a blue onion dome surmounted by a gold ball and a horse, making a visible pun on the owner's name. To keep his workmen contented and at top production during the cold and dark New

England winters, he piped steam heat to all his workshops and installed gaslights to aid the precision work of his artisans.

Protecting his little empire from spring floods, a two-mile dike enclosed most of the two hundred acres. Not one to let a possible profit escape, Colt planted French osier willows along the top of the dike. The fast-growing trees not only stabilized the dike with their roots but also produced a rapidly replaced crop of supple branches suitable for making wicker furniture.

From Potsdam, Germany, Colt brought a colony of skilled wicker-furniture makers. He installed them inside the dike in two-family brick houses of Germanic architecture, built a beer garden, and supported a uniformed oompah band. For all his workers, he built Charter Oak Hall, a meeting place holding one thousand persons. He sponsored dances, concerts, lectures —even the occasional serious meeting, so long as it had no Republican Party overtones, because Colt was a ferociously dedicated Democrat often accused of firing any workmen suspected of sympathy for abolitionists or Republicans. Not that he was proslavery; he just didn't want folks disturbing a stable and profitable status quo.

Colt looked about him and felt it was time to take his rightful place in respectable Hartford society. For that maneuver, he had to shed his image as a hard-drinking and slightly disreputable bachelor. He found a suitable candidate for a wife in Elizabeth Jarvis, eminently respectable as the daughter of Rev. William Jarvis, of Middletown, Connecticut.

The forty-two-year-old bachelor persuaded the thirty-year-old Elizabeth to make socially acceptable his newly won financial prominence on the Hartford scene. Colt made plans to dazzle the city, to impress on it that he had, indeed, arrived.

On June 5, 1856, the steamboat *Washington Irving* tied up at the dike around the armory. Colt and his friends marched from the bunting-draped armory through an immense throng of the curious and well-wishers, greeted the armory band, which was pumping out Teutonic nuptial airs, received a 12-gun salute from his workers (appropriately fired with Colt repeating rifles) from the cupola of the armory, trooped aboard the steamboat, and sailed downriver to Middletown and his bride.

Though he was a Congregationalist, Colt could not pass up the social coup of being married by the Protestant Episcopal bishop of Connecticut.

After the ceremony and the parties, the couple took the train for New York, there to board the *Baltic* for a six-month combined honeymoon and, naturally, business trip to Europe. For some baffling reason, Colt took along as guests the bride's brother and sister, though in-laws are usually as welcome on a honeymoon trip as a fractured pelvis.

Colt felt able to leave his affairs in the competent hands of Root and the rest of his staff, for his business was booming. The armory was turning out 250 finished revolvers a day to feed a ravenous market—especially on the western frontier.

XIII

Indian and border troubles had prompted the re-establishment of the Texas Rangers as an irregular quasi-military mounted police. The group had captured the imagination of the world: even in the Highlands of Scotland a folk song celebrated Ranger service on the Texas frontier.

An English military man wrote a letter to the London *Times* assessing a body he called the American cavalry, clearly the Texas Rangers:

> The Americans as cavalry: —Their seat on horseback, the trotting propensity of the people, the hard mouths of their horses, and the impossibility of bringing them on their haunches render a charge of cavalry in America a pleasant sight to see. . . . But, sir, the Mexicans found it a very unpleasant charge to feel. The reason is obvious;

the Americans armed their cavalry not with the useless carbine, but with the terrible revolving pistol, and by dint of that fearful weapon and the daring gallantry of their race, they cut to pieces a better disciplined cavalry than themselves; and towards the close of the war, the Mexican dragoons could not be brought to face the irregular but dangerous troopers of the United States.

The so-called cavalry vaunted in this letter, especially since they are called irregulars, must have been the Texas Rangers, for there was no cavalry in the United States Army, only dragoons, and the only horse soldiers who charged on horseback—indeed, the only ones armed with Colts—were the Rangers and the Mounted Rifles led by Rangers.

The letter writer proposed taking off the iron breastplates of the British Life Guards as useless and interfering with firing of even the useless carbine. He suggested sending the breastplates to the Crimea so the soldiers there could use them for roasting coffee.

Not all the adventures of the Rangers brought luster to their name.

On the Mexican side of the Rio Grande lived a band of Seminoles who had been evicted from Florida. The Republic had given land to the chieftain, Wild Cat, on his promise to guard the border against gringos, for Mexico was going through a period of turmoil and the country was ruled by local war lords unable to police the long frontier.

True to their tradition of hospitality for the runaway—the very word Seminole means runaway—the Seminoles took in any fugitive slaves who managed to cross the Rio Grande.

Captain James Hughes Callahan, of the Texas Rangers, appears to have lost some of his own slaves to the Seminoles. On patrol with his Ranger company, he met a soldier of fortune named William R. Henry and a band of questionable followers. Henry persuaded Callahan that his duty was to cross into Mexico to recover the runaways. The combined parties numbered 130, every man armed with at least one Colt.

In Mexico a peon tried to warn Callahan that Indians and runaway blacks under Wild Cat had set up an ambush along his road, but the Texan ignored the lowly Mexican. Wild Cat sprang the trap and severely mauled the invaders. They fell back into Piedras Negras, on the Mexican shore. Somebody set fire to the town, and under cover of the smoke, the Texans escaped across the river, but not before looting the town.

The state dismissed Callahan from Ranger service, and the federal government paid Mexico fifty thousand dollars in damages.

No qualified observers reported on the battle, so history does not show how the Seminoles and blacks were armed, but the battle of Piedras Negras marks the first time Rangers had been routed since they discovered Colt's revolvers. Though the force was obviously made up of ruffians, nobody has ever accused the frontier bad man of cowardice. The only conclusion is that the merchant adventurer David Torrey had done only too well south of the border, and Mexicans were becoming as well armed as Texans.

One Indian battle on the High Plains of the Texas Panhandle demonstrated the flaw in the thinking of ordnance officers who persisted in resisting repeaters because they were good only for individual combat. Frontier battles were exactly that—a swirl of individual duels fought collectively.

A brilliant frontiersman—surgeon, surveyor, attorney, journalist, and politician—named John Salmon Ford and known universally as Rip, returned from another quixotic attempt to set up a slave empire in Mexico to accept a commission as captain of Rangers.

With 101 Rangers and 114 Brazos Reserve Indians he patrolled far beyond his authorized area, looking for trouble. A Kichai Indian scout found a Comanche hunting camp; two Indians escaped to warn a large village three miles off. The Comanches rode out, led by a Chief Iron Jacket, so called because he wore a coat of chain mail probably abandoned by one of Coronado's men two centuries earlier.

The battle opened with Chief Iron Jacket, confident in the protection of his armor, riding between the forces to taunt the enemy. Two Indians brought him down with rifle shots.

Ford's own words give the key to understanding frontier warfare:

> The fight was now general, and extended very soon over a circuit of six miles in length and more than three in breadth. It was, in fact, almost a series of single combats.

The Comanches tried to make a stand, but they could not face Ranger and reservation-Indian firepower.

> The din of battle had rolled back from the river—the groans of the dying, cries of frightened women and children, mingled with the reports of firearms, and the shouts of men as they rose from hill top, from thicket, and from ravine.
>
> The second chief had rushed into the conflict with the friendly Indians. A shot from the Shawnee captain Chulle-qua closed his career. The Comanches between the camp and the river were all killed or driven from the field, and our red allies sent up a wild shout of triumph.
>
> The din of battle had alarmed the Comanche warriors of an-

other village. They sent a powerful war party to relieve their cousins—a war party armed with weapons once dominant on western battlefields but rendered obsolete by the Colt revolver. Ford described the Comanche war party as a pageant of "Shields and lances, and bows, and headdresses, and prancing steeds."

Comanches and friendly Indians clashed with little effect. When the Rangers charged to reinforce their Indian allies, the Comanches fled.

Farther north, in the territories of Kansas and Nebraska, beginning in 1854, proslavery and abolitionist forces clashed for seven years before the whole nation began the Civil War. Among the guerillas of both sides who raided opposition towns and outlying settlements, it was common practice to carry several Colts. Some reportedly carried four loaded Colts at once.

In a prolonged brawl such as a Kansas border raid, even a Colt repeater was eventually emptied. The time necessary to reload could be fatal. The obvious solution was to carry more than one loaded pistol. The pony-express riders, to cut weight, rode with a single pistol and a spare cylinder.

During the first few decades of use of revolvers in the West, the two-gun man was not an ambidextrous gunslinger, as he is usually portrayed in moving pictures and television; he was a prudent man who carried a reserve of ready-loaded ammunition in case of misfire or premature exhaustion of the primary weapon. With the advent of metallic cartridges, much more sure of fire than the cap-and-ball and easier to reload, most armed men were content with the burden of a single gun.

During those turbulent pre-Civil War years, one of the most ardent of promoters for Colt rifles and revolvers was George Catlin, who had become famous as a portraitist of the Plains Indians and chronicler of life among the Plains tribes. Colt commissioned the artist to paint scenes of Colts used as hunting weapons in exotic lands drawn from Catlin's many travels. The paintings show a horseman at full gallop firing a revolver into a buffalo; another picking off a string of rheas, the Argentine ostrich; a dramatic scene of Catlin with his rifle running off a pair of jaguars threatening a sleeping camp in Brazil's jungle; a massacre of Texas flamingos with a repeating shotgun; rescue of a companion treed by a herd of angry peccaries; and a final scene of a great powwow of South American Indians stunned by Catlin's demonstration of rapid fire with seven closely spaced puffs of smoke still hanging over the camp.

Colt had lithographs made of several of the paintings and used them in a vigorous advertising campaign to capture the sporting trade. A traveler writing in the mid-1850s from Georgetown, in what is now Guyana, on the northern coast of South America, proves that the scene in the Indian camp was authentic:

> Catlin had one of Colt's pistols in his belt and one of his revolving rifles always in his hand and I had let out the idea that his gun could shoot all day without reloading which made an illustration necessary. The Indians were all anxious to see it set in motion. I placed the door of our hut, which was part of a cowskin stretched on a hoop, at the distance of sixty or seventy yards. The whole village had assembled and Catlin took his position and went off—one! two three four five six. I then stepped up and told him that was enough, I presumed; and while the old chief was assuring him that they were all convinced, and it was a pity to waste any more ammunition, he was slipping the empty cylinder off and another one on, with six charges more, and without their observing what he was doing. He

offered to proceed but all were satisfied that his gun would shoot all day without stopping and this report traveled ahead of us to all the tribes we afterwards visited in that region.

Catlin had named his rifle "Sam." He wrote of himself in Argentina, "I . . . with 'Sam' in hand and a six-shot revolver in my belt, was considered equal to a war party."

Colt encouraged the circulation of any kind of anecdote that boosted his weapon. One frontier tale concerned a Texas judge named Three Leg Williamson because he used a crutch to help his polio-weakened legs. His infirmity had not kept Three Leg from becoming one of the wildest of the Ranger captains in pre-annexation days, and he presided on the bench with stern authority.

According to the tale, a lawyer offered a point of law and the judge asked him for his citation: "Your law, sir, give us the book and page, sir."

"This is my law, sir," said the frontier lawyer, pulling a single-shot horse pistol, "and this, sir, is my book," drawing a bowie knife, "and that is my page," pointing the pistol at the judge.

The judge reached under the bench, drew out a six-shooter, and pointed it at the lawyer's head.

"Your law is not good, sir. The proper authority is *Colt on Revolvers.*"

Across the Pacific, Colt's weapons had found a welcome reception among the Japanese nobles and leaders who received gifts from Commodore Perry. When he returned to the United States, Commodore Perry deposited all gifts from the Japanese with the Navy Department in Washington. Colt heard about them and applied for his share. Commodore Perry wrote Secretary of the Navy J. C. Dobbin:

> My attention has recently been called to two copies of Japanese swords brought home in the *Plymouth* and to an application made by Mr. Samuel Colt that they should be delivered to him.
>
> With reference to the subject, I may remark that Mr. Colt placed in my hands for presentation to whomsoever I might select, more than a thousand dollars worth of his patented pistols and each in a handsome case, of these, besides other arms placed at my disposal by the Government. And I presented a number to the Emperor and Princes of Japan. In return, various presents were sent by the Emperor, and addressed to me all of which that have come to hand have been forwarded to Washington, and among them the arms referred to, although I have no positive proof of the fact, I was led to believe that the arms were intended as return presents for the pistols for Mr. Colt, and so I informed that gentleman. It appears as above stated, that he has applied for them, and it rests with the Department to determine whether, under the circumstances, they can be so disposed of. I cheerfully relinquish any claim I may have upon them and really think that in consideration of the liberality of Mr. Colt he should have them.

The shipment of gifts to Sam included some matchlock muskets of several calibers that showed exquisite workmanship but placed the Japanese gunsmith's art about two centuries behind Colt's.

On June 4, 1856, James again split with his brother, writing, "The object of this letter is to give you notice that I withdraw

from all communication with you. . . . I forgive you for this
last act of your sublime cruelty in attack of my character." Apparently he had suffered no injury since moving to Hartford but
had merely been brooding about his fancied losses in England
and proposed to get a fair settlement through a court of law.

The letter from James breaking off their partnership caught
up with the honeymooning Sam in London. He wrote his plant
manager, Milton Joslin:

> I am greave almost to deth at his consomate folleys & I
> cannot bring my mind to beleeve he is in his senses. . . .
> You must take grate care while you act with firmnes to
> give him as little caus to believe you would do him a personal injury as possable & that you act towards him simply
> in the usual way of business. Should Judg Colt carrey out
> his threts about suipts at law against me or the Company
> then the Company must levey at once upon all the property he has.

Colt had been dickering with Russian officers about building
machines for their arsenals. Also he apparently was still trying
to unload some of those dubiously acquired muskets that General Talcott and Landers had urged him to sell abroad at 7 per
cent commission. So Colt took his bridal party to St. Petersburg, capital of the Czar.

From the American embassy in Russia, on August 18, 1856,
Colt sent to his plant manager a notice of the presentation to
the court of himself and his party. With the eagerness of the
rankest *arriviste,* he ordered his manager to send it to the local
paper and ask them to "publish it in French as it is or in inglish
. . . . but be shure to have the notice coped in the Times and
current to enlighten our friends. . . ."

Colt said that he and his brother-in-law Richard Jarvis had

been attached to the United States legation for the coronation of the Czar in Moscow on September 7, 1856, and would travel there on a special train for the diplomatic corps. He reported with a regrettable note of toadying to European aristocracy that the American women would occupy the same "high places as those aloted to the most distinguished lades of the grate countries who are represented here on this sublime occasion. . . ."

Charles Caesar, of the London plant, and a few skilled workmen accompanied a shipment of three thousand Navy pistols to Moscow, and on September 3, 1856, Colt joined them for a solemn inspection. Colt wrote an angry letter to Hartford:

> . . . Mr. Cezar has examined the arms & reports them to be the very wirst lot of arms he has seen made at the Hartford Armoury. I am afraid there is grose neglect in the fitting & inspection departments at home & *I wish you to call Mr. Roots special attention to the matter atonce & correct the evil.*

He also reported that work had gone so slack in London that several "Yankey boys" had gone home. Colt urged his manager to find work for them, because he did not "want to loose sight of them in cace they are again wanted in Europe & furthermore I had much rather keep old hands employed who have been faithful."

Colt's concern about his faithful workers and the obvious decline of his London business make James Colt's petition to the Superior Court of Connecticut on September 4, 1856, sound ungrateful, pretentious, querulous, and highly questionable in the facts he cited.

He said he was lured away from St. Louis to England with a promise to split profits from the English Armory, his share to be one hundred thousand dollars. He discovered there were no profits. To induce him to stay, Sam promised him a half interest in the tools, machinery, and stock, according to James; so he returned to England and ran the plant, this time for a profit.

James further said that Sam had doctored the books to conceal the four-hundred-thousand-dollar profit that had accrued only because of James's good management. The value of the stock and tools he set at another two hundred thousand dollars. He asked for a division of properties. The court submitted the case to arbitration.

Colt had acquired enough property to tempt any litigious ex-partner. The New York *Journal of Commerce,* on August 30, 1856, estimated the value of buildings and machinery at the Hartford plant at $1 million, employees at about 500 with a monthly payroll of $15,000 to $20,000 with production of 150 to 200 pistols a day, all big figures for the era. The article described offices, machine shop, engine rooms, blacksmith shop, iron and brass foundries, storerooms, shooting gallery, and fifty dwellings for workmen, the whole "erected on a tract of land embracing 150 acres, formerly inundated by the Connecticut River, but now enclosed by two miles of strong dyke."

Dwarfing the 30-horsepower English steam engine that had so impressed Charles Dickens, the Hartford engine was of 350 horsepower, with a flywheel thirty feet across. Belts conveyed power from engine to machines with none of the noise of gear drives:

> For this reason a strange sensation is experienced on entering the immense apartment used for the armory, which presents an unbroken area 500 feet in length by 60 in breadth, completely filled with machinery, and not less than 200 men engaged in operating it, all in rapid motion, yet comparative quiet prevails. It is believed that nowhere,

in any country, can another shop be found of equal extent occupied by such an amount of machinery.

The reporter expanded on the beauty of the machinery and the complexity of the operations it performed:

The larger portion of it is the invention of E. K. Root. . . .

The article reported that the Hartford plant had already made 185,296 pistols, of four models.

The London works displayed no such bustle, however, and Colt closed it, in December 1856, except for service and repairs. Total production in the four years of operation was about forty-eight thousand pistols, all but eight thousand during the Crimean War years.

A short time later, on February 24, 1857, Elizabeth bore their first child, a son, who lived only a few months.

And Colt was by no means rid of his first family, overseas. Caroline, alias Julia, had met Count Friedrich August Kunow Waldemar von Oppen, a Prussian cavalry officer and son of a landed Prussian nobleman. The father had become alarmed at his son's attentions to a woman he considered a vulgar adventuress. He wrote his son a letter. It begins with the stiff salutation "Sir":

I will purchase an estate for you in the province of Silesia, and give you the entire use of it during your own life, with the condition that at your death the property with all its appurtenances and any revenues or moneys belonging to it be returned to me by your wife or children, male or female. If you do not wish to become a landed proprietor, and wish to remain in the army, I will give you

10,000 thalers for your military wants, with the condition that at your death your wife may not have the use of it. If you wish I shall take care of the 10,000 thalers and pay you the interest of it every three months, with the condition that you give me your word of honor that this quarterly revenue is for your own private use and for your expenses as a military man, and that your wife does not share in it directly or indirectly.

The old man voiced his suspicion of the woman's relationship with Colt:

If Colonel Colt is a relative of hers he can make some provision for his own ward, if he is no relation of hers and if she was not his ward, then she deserves to be cut out of all privileges as an inheritress of your property. . . . Who is she? Who were her parents? Why did every one of her guardian's compatriots turn her into ridicule and neglect her openly?

He cast doubt on the marriage certificate Caroline apparently carried to justify Samuel Junior's existence:

Was it from real distress, or modesty, in the church vestry, or from affectation, that her hands became powerless when she took the pen to sign her marriage certificate?

He noted that she had paled when he asked about her father and had become hysterical when his wife asked about Caroline's mother:

Why does young Sam stare in such an idiotic manner when asked if he remembers his parents? And if Colonel Colt loved Julia as a ward, or if she was worth loving and caring for, why did he leave her in Germany to find a home? . . .

Caroline wrote Sam asking for a loan to set her fiancé up in business. Sam advanced them one thousand dollars and made Von Oppen an agent of the company. (The young aristocrat, incidentally, turned out to be an excellent businessman and stayed with the company till long after Colt's death.) He wrote the young man about his approaching marriage to Caroline and reported that he had asked his friend, the American consul in London, to attend the wedding as his representative:

I have endeavored to so fix my business so that I could go to London and attend the sacred ceremony but it is quite impossible and I must therefore finally disappoint Julia and yourself in this particular but I shall be with you in spirit and my blessings shall attend you both.

His letter then goes into an arch appreciation of their wish for privacy after the ceremony and compares it to his own flight from society to be alone with his bride the year before—apparently forgetting that his bride's brother and sister were cozily present throughout the honeymoon trip. The letter has a complacent and avuncular tone extraordinary for a man marrying off his legal wife to another man for the second time.

Sam also sent one hundred English pounds to his agent in Berlin to pay Junior's tutor. Reports of his schooling remained bad, however, and Colt soon had him sent home and entered in a private school in Boston.

James's lawsuit turned out well for Sam. The arbitration board found that Sam owed James $5,897.50, but that, on the other hand, James owed Sam $10,184.49, leaving a net debt of James to Sam of $4,286.99. James sold out his possessions in

Hartford. His agent offered to sell the cottage on Weatherfield Street to Sam, but Sam replied he had "no desire now again to own the house he gave Judge Colt."

And on the frontier, the soldiers still complained about their armament—not that they didn't have revolvers but that they had only one each.

Lieutenant John B. Hood, of the 2d Cavalry, who as a Confederate general only eight years later would oppose Sherman's march to the sea through Georgia, reported to the New York *Times* in late 1857 that once while on patrol he saw horsemen bearing a white flag. He supposed them to be friendly Tonkawa Indians and allowed them to approach. At a signal ten mounted Indians and an undetermined number on foot attacked with rifles, bows, and lances. Concentrated fire of six-shooters drove them back (one cavalryman hung his rifle on the cantle of his saddle to give his revolver greater scope). When the weapons were empty they fell back to reload:

> If I had two six-shooters to a man I would have killed and wounded nearly all of them. In the engagement I killed nine and wounded ten or twelve.

He suffered one killed, one missing, and one wounded, himself and three others slightly wounded. Reinforcements arrived, and they searched for the war party, with no luck.

XIV

To open the New Year of 1858, Samuel Colt petitioned Congress to grant him a second extension of his basic patent of February 25, 1836. His petition gives an admirable summary of his career as inventor and arms maker. His argument for extension was ingenious:

> . . . it is the policy of the law to give to every inventor the exclusive right to and full enjoyment of his invention for the term of fourteen years; that by reason of circumstances, wholly beyond the control of your petitioner, instead of receiving any profit from the use of his invention during the term of fourteen years, he sustained an actual loss; and that although his said patent was extended for the term of seven years for his benefit, during that period of time, by reason of the great cost of machinery to manu-

2

facture the said arms of a suitable quality to insure safety
to the public in the use of them, the profit received from
the manufacture and sale of the said arms having been expended in the machinery for their improved construction,
there remains to your petitioner no real available profits
thus far from his invention, unless, by an extension of his
patent, his accumulated machinery and tools can be kept
employed; and to do which by the means asked for, is
awarding to your petitioner but a very small part of the
value of his invention to the public.

One E. S. Boyd filed a counterpetition before the House
Committee on Patents citing vast profits to Colt, who

maliciously renews such application from time to time
backed by great wealth and influence. . . . Your remonstrant is fully convinced that said Colt has made over three
millions of dollars from the monopoly he has enjoyed, and
remonstrates against further extension thereof.

Your remonstrant will be glad to furnish at far less
prices than now demanded by said Colt, of a quality equal
or better than his, and from his models which your remonstrant contends are now the right and property of the
public.

Admirably persuasive as Colt's petition was, he had no
confidence in its acceptance on merit alone. Colt set in motion
the old Washington grease machine.

On May 10, 1858, Colt's clerk J. D. Alden wrote Sam asking
for five thousand dollars, to be returned if the committee did
not report favorably:

If it is in your favor on the terms proposed, the money will go to the parties who buy this "blackmail" and who they are I have not the slightest idea.

Three days later, he wrote that he had called on an unnamed committee member who was ill in bed. Alden said he had hinted all about the point with little immediate success:

I found, my dear Colonel, that he was very cautious and would not give me a chance to ask him for a proposition it being so delicate a subject for me to act upon that I dared not on your account as well as my own propose a thing to him.

The committee member kindled some hope in Alden, however, by suggesting that if Colt meant to change the mind of any committee members he should be in Washington the next week:

It looked to me as though someone might be induced to change and to *my mind he was the man.*

The Secretary of War, John Floyd, wrote Representative James A. Stewart, chairman of the Committee on Patents:

With "Colt's pistol" the country is perfectly familiar; it is agreed on all hands, by those who have used them in the field . . . that it is altogether superior to any other, and in fact it has now become essential to the public service. . . .

Patents are granted for the encouragement of an inventive ingenuity which is intended finally to result in the benefit of the public, as well as to the comfort and convenience of the people. Mr. Colt's invention has worked out a result peculiar to it alone, as far as my knowledge goes.

Secretary Floyd stated that Colt had not only doubled the

efficiency of mounted troops on the frontier but had also built an armory "which rises to the importance of a great national work." The Hartford plant, Floyd said, was superior in machinery and extent to either of the national armories. It was in fact the largest armory in the world:

> In case of any public necessity this armory of Mr. Colt's could be turned to great and essential advantage in arming our people. It is a matter of some moment, therefore, that this armory should be sustained and placed on a permanent footing, if it can be certainly done without cost to the Government, or violation of a sound policy.

Colt affixed a report of the faithful General Harney:

> I consider the arm perfect for the dragoon service, particularly when opposed to the Western Prairie Indians. It is the only weapon with which we can hope ever to subdue those wild and daring tribes. . . .

Referring again to his Seminole War campaign, General Harney closed with:

> I honestly believe that but for these arms the Indians would now be luxuriating in the everglades of Florida.

The Ordnance Department, however, remained true to the Talcott tradition. On November 1, 1858, the ordnance chief, Colonel H. K. Craig, filed a report on arming the militia:

> . . . the rifle muskets of the model of 1855 . . . will have a beneficial effect, as the high finish and attractive appearance of the arm will not only encourage a military spirit in the militia, but will tend to counteract efforts that are being made to induce requisitions from state authorities for arms of private manufacture, that are more suita-

ble for predatory warfare and personal rencountres than for the use of the militia of the country. . . .

Again, Colt was harassed by the parade mentality of the desk soldier, who preferred the smart appearance of a shiny single-shot musket to the devastating firepower of a repeating pistol.

His comment about "predatory warfare" did have its pertinence to the situation in Texas. Senator Sam Houston introduced a bill in Congress providing that the United States establish a protectorate over Mexico. He privately approached Colonel Robert E. Lee, proposing to name him Protector of Mexico if he would back Houston for President of the United States. He wrote letters to Secretary Floyd asking permission to raise a large force of Texas Rangers and did indeed scratch together almost one thousand Rangers, the largest size the force would be in its entire history. Houston planned a "liberating" force of five thousand Rangers armed with rifles and six-shooters—at federal expense, of course. It didn't work out, somehow.

Sam could not respond to Houston's grandiose plans as he might have at one time, for he suffered increasingly from gout, an illness so painful it requires the full concentration of the patient.

Late in 1858, Colt and Elizabeth and their infant son Caldwell moved into Armsmear, the perfect model of a Victorian-age mogul's idea of opulence and elegance, all towers, porticoes, gingerbread, and the other architectural gimcrackery affected by the financial barons of the day. Sam increasingly lingered at his desk in the great mansion, running the barony from a distance and allowing more and more detail to slip into the hands of his extraordinarily able staff.

He did rouse himself sufficiently to write on January 2, 1859, to General Kingman, in Washington:

> My dear General
> I sent by express today a half Dozzen boxes Champagne, 4 of Quarts and Too of Pint Bottles with the compliments of the season & the cause of Patent extention.

Sam's raw efforts at bribery were mostly from long habit. Except for the understandably hostile testimony of would-be competitors before the House Patent Committee, the public reports on Colt's arms were good.

On February 21, 1859, Secretary Floyd submitted to the Senate a report from a board of army officers appointed to determine the most economical and efficient arms for United States mounted troops on the frontier. With Brevet Brigadier General W. S. Harney presiding, a favorable report was a foregone conclusion:

> The board recommend the adoption of Colt's pistol (with breech attachment) and ammunition for the cavalry service, and that each trooper be furnished with two pistols, adjusted to the same breech, the barrel of each pistol to be eight inches long, of the calibre of the army revolver. . . . The board . . . also reccomend that the pistol be sighted for one, two and three hundred yards.

Sam had designed a means of mounting a rifle stock on the butt of his pistols to convert them to a kind of repeating carbine. Hence the sighting for the tremendous range of three hundred yards:

> The board recommend that one pistol be worn on the right side of the soldier, in a pouch attached to the sabre belt, and the other in the holster on the right side of the

saddle, and that the breech attachment be carried in a suitable pouch attached to the left side of the rear of the saddle.

The board agreed to accept seven-inch barrels if the eight-inchers were not ready for an approaching Indian campaign.

Colonel Craig also submitted an estimate of cost for 8,500 pistols and ammunition to arm five regiments: $270,436.

Colt had written his agent in Washington that he was willing to pay out fifty thousand dollars after the patent extension became law ("this same should be equalley divided between the Republicans & Democrats") but his failing health and the booming market for weapons regardless of patent protection caused him to drop the effort, and the drive for renewal quietly came to a halt.

On April 28, 1859, Lieutenant Hans Busk, of the Victoria Rifles, British Army, sent Colt a target riddled with pistol balls. He enclosed a testimonial:

[Colt's] cavalry pistols are, in fact, pocket rifles. With one of them I . . . fired from a rest, at the Erith rifle ground, thirty-six rounds at the enormous range of FOUR HUNDRED AND TEN YARDS! Six bullets struck the butt at distances varying from thirty to thirty-six inches from the center of the target, eighteen bullets struck within the circumference of a circle seven feet in diameter and the other six shots at heights varying from ten to twelve feet above the target—satisfactorily proving the capacity of the weapon for a still greater range. . . .

(Six shots are unaccounted for by Lieutenant Busk, but the score remains impressive, considering the tremendous range, a totally impractical range for a pistol.)

Lieutenant Busk added a note about the Colt revolver:

> Considering that I have fired more than 68,000 rounds
> from my own shoulder my opinion in such matters is per-
> haps worth more than the mere empty praise of a green
> hand; let any one who wants to know what a Colt can do
> take my word that for efficiency and strength of shooting
> nothing can beat it.

Overseas, Caroline's husband, Von Oppen, was deeply embroiled in the power politics that kept nineteenth-century Mit-
teleuropa in perpetual turmoil. Austria was at war with an alliance of the Kingdom of Sardinia and France; Russia and
Prussia were arming on the sidelines. Von Oppen tried to resign
his commission but was refused. On June 16, 1859, he wrote
from Bonn that he had been called to active duty in the Prussian Cavalry. He continued moonlighting for Colt:

> I am trying to introduce the Colt pistol into my regi-
> ment and have made a beginning by selling until now in all
> about fifteen (15) Navy pistols to my brother-officers
> here; some of them were already in possession of these pis-
> tols.

The originals of these letters from the German, Von Oppen,
to the semiliterate Sam Colt are remarkable for their distinguished hand and limpid English.

Von Oppen did not believe he would be involved in combat:

> . . . Our army is only put on a footing of war merely to
> give more weight to our diplomatic negotiations. And to
> scare the French, if possible. . . .

He guessed correctly, for by late August 1859 he was disbanding his troops because of decreasing tension following a
peace treaty between Austria and the Allies.

In the United States, there was no talk of disbanding troops, for tension between North and South increased daily. John Brown's raid on Harpers Ferry, on October 16, 1859, and his effort to arm a slave uprising did little to calm southern nerves. Southern states began arming militia, and southern gentlemen began arming themselves. One of Sam's friends wrote after a trip through the South that "men are casting quantities of lead into bullets. I heard a Southerner from Alabama say he had two barrles full in his cellar. A rise in pig lead may be expected."

Not one to miss a market, regardless of the use his arms might be put to, Sam contracted with a relative, Amos Colt, to travel through the southern and southwestern states. Amos was a droll fellow and wrote amusing letters:

> From Mississippi. They are all horsemen here. They are too damn lazy to walk. Southern gentlemen live upon fare that the humblest mechanic would turn up his nose at in the North then sell their cotton in the fall or a nigger and then splurge around the St. Charles [hotel in New Orleans] with a beautiful pair of boots and rich gloves the rest of the suit looks as if they had bivouaced in them for twelve months. Let her rip. Yours on hog and hominy.

A correspondent wrote the *Daily Express* from Baton Rouge, Louisiana:

> . . . Mr. Amos Colt, an agent of the famous Colonel Sam, of revolver notoriety has been here for the past week, exhibiting the Colt revolver and musket, the artillery sword bayonet, rifle and other arms for the inspection of the Governor and members of the legislature. It is proposed to adopt the Colt revolving musket for the State Military Academy near Alexandria and to furnish our military companies with the same.

A shooting match came off here yesterday between
Mr. A. H. Colt and Mr. H. Bernard of West Baton Rouge
who is considered one of the best shots in the state. The
weapons were shotguns, Mr. Colt using his revolving shotgun. They first shot at bottles thrown in the air and then at
two billiard balls, one thrown to the right and the other to
the left, Mr. Colt accomplishing the feat of hitting both
balls before they commenced to descend. The next feat was
to hit a five cent piece also thrown into the air. It is needless
to say Mr. Colt beat his adversary and was eminently successful.

The tone of the report on the shooting match could bring on
the suspicion that Amos, taking a lesson from the old master of
public relations, Sam Colt, had written the dispatch himself.

The Hartford paper reported seeing at the express office
addressed to Harpers Ferry, Virginia:

ten boxes of Sharp's rifles, six boxes of rifle ammunition,
four cases of Colt's revolvers and four cases of pistol ammunition.

So it seems the Virginians are not too proud to use
Yankee made rifles and Yankee made powder and ball.

Three days later the paper carried a ponderously sarcastic
letter about an order from the governor of Virginia for four
hundred revolving rifles to arm his brave army against a hypothetical cow and calf that had supposedly frightened his militia:

The cost of the arms will be about twenty thousand
dollars—a good days trade.

From the New York *Herald* came a story reporting Colt as
having made a generous gesture, uncharacteristic in that it
could have undermined a possible sale. At a meeting in New

York's St. Nicholas Hotel, Colt presented to a committee of Italian patriots one hundred cavalry pistols for use by Garibaldi in his battle to free and unify Italy.

Irish newspapers about the same time carried notices of the bark *C. B. Troit,* with a manifest showing 23,500 muskets consigned to Colt's agent Dennett in London but actually destined for Garibaldi as a gift from American sympathizers. The Wexford *Constitution* doubted the generosity of Americans because of indifference to Garibaldi's cause and suggested the muskets had been bought secretly with British money. Dennett protested the muskets were an honest "mercantile adventure," and he did advertise them for sale in *La Presse.*

From the Missouri River, Colt received an order for a revolving rifle from Lieutenant J. E. B. Stuart, of the 1st Cavalry Regiment, who was to die in the cavalry action at Yellow Tavern in 1864 after having dazzled the world for three years by riding his troopers completely around Union armies whenever the tactical situation required a swift reconnaissance. He had been with Colonel Robert E. Lee at the suppression of John Brown's raid just a few weeks before he wrote the order to Colt, but was already in Kansas preparing a campaign against the Plains Indians. His order was welcome but not tactful:

> I want one of your own selection which you can warrant *not* to fire but one barrel at a *time.*

Colt and Root were working on a new pistol design. Knowing that the War Department was preparing an order to equip five regiments of cavalry with the Dragoon model, Colt wrote Secretary of War John Floyd on May 10, 1860, that he was making "important changes and improvements," which he wanted a board of officers to consider before he proceeded with a large government order.

The Dragoon, at .44 caliber, was a weapon carrying a tremendous wallop, but the huge pistol's weight wore down all but the most powerful marksmen. Colt and Elisha Root undertook to maintain the punch but trim the weight of the cavalry's favorite weapon. By retaining the caliber size while drastically cutting the powder charge, they were able to work economies in steel that cut the weight to 2 pounds 11 ounces, only slightly more than modern pistols weigh. Dubbed the New Model Army Pistol, the weapon had a beautiful balance and smooth action.

A board of officers, on May 18, 1860, announced results of a test competition between the Dragoon and the New Model:

> The superiority of Colt's revolvers, as an arm for cavalry service, which has been so well established, is now finally confirmed by the production of the new model with the 8 inch barrel. There are a few minor points requiring modification, to which the manufacturer's notice has been called, and to which he should be required to attend in any arms of the kind he may furnish for Government use . . . the Board are satisfied that the New Model Revolver with the 8 inch barrel will make the most superior cavalry arm we have ever had and they recommend the adoption of this New Model and its issue to all the mounted troops.

Chairman of that board was J. E. Johnston, who only months later would resign his commission to join the Confederacy and make a record as the best defensive general the South had.

The enthusiastic approval of the board marked the acceptance by all but a few mossbacks in the military of the revolver as the principal cavalry arm. A few holdouts persisted. In California, General James H. Carlton reserved fifty sabers for the best-mounted and most-expert horsemen of his cavalry. He made an inspirational speech:

Have your sabers sharp, very sharp, that they may readily cut through clothing . . . The cold steel will still win against the pistol.

Fortunately for General Carlton's saber-wielding troopers, in their Civil War service they never had to face a charge by mounted Texans armed with Colt revolvers.

While the nation was arming itself, North and South, for the tragic war about to erupt, Colt, despite his illness, had turned his attention to a new venture, in Arizona.

In late 1859 he had bought one thousand shares of the Sonora Exploring and Mining Company to operate a silver mine that had been worked by the Spaniards and mission Indians decades before but abandoned because their mining technology was not far enough advanced for the depth of the shaft. Sam paid for his shares half in bank drafts, half in pistols for resale at the company store.

Mine headquarters were at Tubac, and the president of the company was Major Samuel Peter Heinzelman, late of the 2d Infantry Regiment, a soldier with a brilliant career on the Rio Grande. Early assay of the ore showed an excitingly high yield.

Though he was already a wealthy industrialist with every prospect of becoming wealthier still through arms manufacture, the promise of the silver mine inflamed Colt. He began maneuvering to gain control. He never lost sight of his basic trade, however, and wrote in 1860 to J. D. Alden, his clerk at the Tubac store:

I am noticing in the newspapers occasionally complimentary notices of the Sharp & Burnside Rifles & Carbines, anecdotes of there use upon Grisley Bares, Indians, Mexecans, &c &c. Now this is all rong it should be pub-

lished Colts Rifles Carbines &c When there is or can be
maid a good storrey of the use of a Colts Revolving Rifle
Carbine Shotgun or Pistol for publication in the Arizzonan
the opertunaty should & in the event of such notices being
published you must always send me one hundred Copes If
there is a chance to du a few good things in this way give
the editor a Pistol or Rifle complement in the way it will
tell You know who to du this & Do not forget to have his
Colums report all the axidents that occur to the Sharps &
other humbug arms.

Perhaps to curry more favor among potential customers, Colt
contributed a well-stocked public library to the community,
probably the first library in Arizona.

Even a good stock of Colts could not hold off depredations
of the rapacious Apaches. The Arizona frontier was so thinly
guarded by federal forces, it was no exaggeration to call it
defenseless. Alden wrote Colt in March of 1860:

. . . unless some protection from Government is granted
. . . the "white man" may as well abandon the country at once. The country is alive with Apaches. It was
only a few days since they killed two of our wood
choppers & drove off thirty head of the company's cattle—
the bodies of the wood choppers were literally filled with
arrows & their heads nearly severed from their bodies with
the axes they had been to work with.

A mixed American-Mexican posse chased the Indians ninety
miles and recovered twenty-four of the cattle.

A shipment of mine machinery and a new engineer—named
Talcott—arrived, but mine production still languished because
of the Indian threat.

The governor of the neighboring Mexican state of Sonora offered a one-hundred-dollar bounty on Apache scalps, and the Pimo and Papago Indians set about an enthusiastic slaughter of their redskin brothers.

Still, Apaches ran off all the horses and mules of the mining company and ambushed the pursuing party, killing one and wounding another.

Colt began quietly unloading his mining stock and redirected his attention to revolvers. By July 1860 he was no longer a mining magnate. The next month, he chartered a steamer and took a cruise in sheltered waters. In October his ten-month-old daughter died, leaving the Colts with only a son, Caldwell—and young Samuel also, of course. The death of his daughter hurt the already enfeebled Colt.

During his mining fling, Colt's attention to his armament business never flagged, for the nation was rushing headlong toward a catastrophic war and Sam meant to profit. Even after southern states began seceding, in late 1860, Colt pushed his arms sales North and South.

To treat his waning health, Colt was forced in early 1861 to turn over the booming business, at least temporarily, to his staff and sail to Cuba for winter warmth and the hot-spring baths. He did not forget business and wrote Hartford on February 18, 1861:

> *Make hay while sun shines* . . . the news we get here from New Orleans is very warlike and I am sure of a market for all the arms we can make whether there is a fight or not.

He urged double shifts to lay in a stock of arms of all sizes and types.

He added a plaintive note of clearly forced optimism about his health:

> The daily heat here is . . . 80 degrees. . . . I still keep on my flannels and most of my thick clothes preparing to take them off while I am taking sulphur baths daily. My health is improving so fast I rarely ever use my crutches now I walk pretty well with the aid of a cane. Should I continue to improve for a fortnight longer, I shall probably pack up and go back to Havana to take the steamer for New Orleans.

Colt did not even have to go to New Orleans to drum up trade. In Hartford, orders for weapons poured in from all parts of the country—and were respectfully filled.

Under pretense of arming Texas against the Indians, Ben McCulloch wrote from San Antonio on February 24, 1861, to say that Texas wished that one thousand to two thousand of the New Model Army be mailed to New Orleans. He asked how to go about paying for them and warned he had to have them by "the first of April or they will be too late for those who take the field against the Indians." No anti-Indian campaign of such magnitude had ever been contemplated, McCulloch himself had already seized the Alamo in the name of what would become the Confederacy, and Texas was deeply committed already to secession. The pistols were clearly meant to arm Texas militia for the approaching war with the Union.

Letters poured in for personal weapons—from Macon, Georgia; Warrens Landing, Missouri; Lexington, Kentucky; Heswick Depot, Virginia; Oxford, Mississippi.

And Colt hastened to fill all orders, regardless of the source. With the hard-bitten cynicism of the true arms peddler, he referred to his arming of both sides of the approaching fratricidal blood bath as "my latest work on 'Moral Reform.'" He openly talked of building armories in the South. Editorial writers at the Hartford *Courant* and the New York *Times* led a parade of journalists who denounced his trading with what they were already calling the enemy.

On March 12, 1861, South Carolina militia fired on Fort Sumter, at Charleston, to force regular-army troops to hand over federal supplies the state government claimed had become state property with secession. On April 15, 1861, President Abraham Lincoln issued his call to arms; the Civil War had begun.

But the embargo on trade with the South came just too late to thwart Sam. His last acknowledged shipment—five hundred guns addressed to Richmond—had just left in boxes prudently labeled "hardware."

The Confederacy was thus officially cut off by the embargo from further direct supply by Colt. Newspaper clippings of the period report, however, that a trade of some kind survived the cutoff, for in 1863 the steamer *George Caldwell* was seized because a search of the hold turned up fifty barrels marked "lard" but stuffed with Colt Navy models. So the Confederacy apparently kept some lines of contact open to Hartford.

In the southland itself Colts remained in fair supply, for factories in Macon, Greensboro, and Atlanta, all in Georgia, and smaller plants elsewhere turned out creditable imitations of Colt Navy revolvers.

The cavalry genius Nathan Bedford Forrest traveled to Louisville, Kentucky, and bought from his pocket—he had become a wealthy man as slave trader and cotton planter—about five hundred Colt revolvers to arm those volunteers wishing to join his mounted regiment but unable to afford private side arms.

In March of 1929 a visitor idly poking about in the ruins of the former Confederate Fort Fisher uncovered a rusty loaded Colt. He pulled the trigger and it fired after at least sixty-four years in the mud and rain. As proof of the desperation of the South to arm itself with Colts, it was an ancient five-shooter. But it had racked up eight notches on the handle before it was lost.

The Hartford armory was bursting with orders. Besides the roaring demand for Navy models as private weapons, the government ordered 387,017 pistols, 113,980 muskets, and almost seven thousand rifles.

Shortly after the call to arms, on April 30, 1861, Colt wrote the Hartford City Council complaining of being taxed at a rate four-and-a-half times the rate of his immediate neighbor. He announced his plan to double the size of his armory but threatened to build it elsewhere unless given tax relief. The city council scrambled to adjust his assessment. Colt began construction within the same dikes that protected the first plant.

Gout and rheumatic fever continued to attack during the summer of 1861. During the Christmas season, the painful disease brought him to bed. By January 4, 1862, he had recovered enough to do a little business from his bed, but tired quickly. He took to reading a Bible his father had given him years before, but his mind began to falter.

Colt became delirious; during occasional lucid intervals he was distressed by the pain he was causing his wife, for he understood he was dying.

"It is all over now," he said and lapsed into a final delirium. On January 10, 1862, Samuel Colt died, aged forty-seven.

Sam would have enjoyed his funeral. The pomp and ceremony would have tickled his vanity—though the idling of the ar-

mory and furniture factory out of respect for the day might
have troubled the businessman in his soul.

The entire work force—at fifteen hundred men, one of the
largest in America—filed by his coffin at Armsmear, wearing
mourning bands on sleeves. After religious services in the parlor, they formed a double line through which passed the Put-
nam Phalanx and Company A, 12th Regiment of Connecticut
Volunteers, their bands beating muffled drums and the riflemen
carrying reversed arms.

Among the eight pallbearers carrying the coffin to his private
burying ground, within the estate, Colt would have been pleased
to see Thomas Seymour, whom he helped elect governor, and
Henry C. Deming, mayor of Hartford.

Hartford had good reason to celebrate the name of their native son. By sheer brass nerve and inventive genius, seasoned by
the moral sense of a Corsican bandit, Samuel Colt had bulled
his way through phalanxes of stupid officials, bribed his way
past armies of venal politicians, cajoled and plotted till he had
created an immense industrial empire, invented a manufacturing
system that would revolutionize the world, and blown out of the
way with his firearms all impediments to the occupation of
present-day continental United States.

By no means as a side benefit, he had also acquired a
fifteen-million-dollar fortune, one of the largest in North America, so that Elizabeth was left with a two-hundred-thousand-
dollar annual income, a stupendous sum for the time. Caldwell
was remembered well in the will and named a vice-president of
the company, though he rarely visited his desk.

Also generously remembered was Samuel Caldwell Colt,
born Samuel Colt, Jr. Elizabeth displayed an almost saintly nature in taking young Sam into her heart with warm affection,
though it was painfully obvious what his true relationship was.

Out of courtesy to the unacknowledged son, she even permitted a portrait of the mysterious Caroline Henshaw, young Sam's acknowledged mother and Sam Senior's first and still undivorced wife. When Samuel Caldwell Colt married, she staged an elaborate wedding at the mansion and moved the couple into a house on the grounds.

Shortly before dying, Sam had handed over his powers to Richard Jarvis, the brother-in-law who had learned something of his business affairs during the honeymoon trip to Russia. With Elisha Root and the rest of the staff, Jarvis went on with the great work of arming a nation for war.

XV

Colt's influence on American history did not end with his death.

It is impossible to assess the share of Civil War carnage worked by Colt's revolvers. They—or revolvers much like them —did, however, become the principal weapon of crack cavalry units. Two of the most dashing cavalry commanders—Nathan Bedford Forrest and John Hunt Morgan dispensed with the traditional saber entirely and relied on pistols.

In one celebrated raid, General Morgan carried his six-shooters deep into Ohio, the farthest penetration of the North by any Confederate commander.

But Forrest could make an even bolder claim for his pistol packers:

On June 10, 1864, Union General S. D. Sturgis left Memphis and marched eight thousand men across northern Mississippi with the mission of breaking up Forrest's band of thirty-three hundred cavalrymen before they could raid Union supply lines in Tennessee. Forrest's scouts reported on the progress of the Union force. The Confederate cavalry genius dismounted his men and deployed them in dense woods flanking the road. Exhausted and thirsty from a brutal march under the Mississippi summer sun, the Union soldiers stumbled into the trap. Forrest's cavalrymen, hidden in the underbrush, poured murderous fire from their Colt Navy six-shooters into the massed Union ranks.

Reeling back, the invader tried to make a stand at the crossroads, but their will collapsed and they fled. Trying to cross Tishomingo Creek, a wagon jammed crossways on the bridge, blocking the retreat.

Total annihilation threatened till a battalion of black soldiers formed a rear defense that stood long enough to let the main body escape.

Brices Cross Roads was the only major battle of the Civil War won almost entirely by revolver firepower.

Though no major battles were fought there after the war's opening skirmishes, in the tragically divided states of Kansas and Missouri the pistol was also the major weapon. Most of the fighting forces were guerilla bands such as the infamous Quantrill's Raiders. Because they used the classic guerilla tactic of striking swiftly and fleeing before the enemy could organize defenses, the irregulars of both sides had to be mounted to foil pursuit. Like regular cavalrymen back east, they had early appreciated the value of the Colt as a horseman's weapon. But they went the regulars at least one better. General Morgan insisted that each of his troopers carry two pistols; the Kansas and Missouri guerillas carried as many as four. The notorious Bloody Bill Anderson carried eight on his person and four more in saddle holsters.

Not that the guerillas did any more fighting than necessary. Their pistols mostly murdered innocent civilians in bloody raids and counterraids on towns suspected of harboring sympathizers with the enemy. These looked far more like bandit forays than acts of war.

The greatest victory won by Quantrill's Raiders, for instance, was a raid in August 1863 on Lawrence, Kansas, where his 450 men butchered every civilian male they could catch, including boys, and set the town aflame. Billy Anderson's bunch, on September 27, 1864, looted Centralia, Missouri, held up a train, seized three thousand dollars, and massacred twenty Union soldiers riding as passengers. By some mishap, they were forced later that day to fight an outnumbered Union body. Their blazing six-shooters almost wiped out the one-shot-musket-wielding pursuers, proving they could fight when forced to.

In general, however, the war record of the guerilla reeks of banditry. Indeed, many of the notorious outlaw chieftains that plagued the nation in postwar years—men such as Frank and Jesse James and Cole Younger—got their training with Quantrill.

Colt armory records show that the company during the Civil War manufactured seven thousand rifles, 113,980 muskets . . . and 387,017 revolvers. The government bought less than half that number of revolvers, so that a prodigious number belonged to soldiers returning to civilian life. (A substantial number of government-owned side arms also disappeared into the civilian mass, for wily veterans in all wars smuggle their side arms home.)

In the turbulent Reconstruction period many Southerners used those side arms to correct real or fancied injustices. Texas came near to outright anarchy. Footloose adventurers from the North drifted westward, most of them armed and many spoiling for trouble. For four war years, a man's worth had been measured by his courage and his willingness to kill. Those values survived the war and gave rise to a generation of reckless gunfighters that worked their craft on both sides of the law, sometimes simultaneously. Though some favored the double-barreled shotgun and some the repeating rifle, the principal weapon of the western gunslinger was the revolver—and almost always a Colt.

Western history bristles with the names of famous *pistoleros:* Billy the Kid, Harry Tracy, Dallas Stoudenmire, Butch Cassidy, the Sundance Kid, and so on in a roll call that has furnished heroes for a seemingly endless stream of romances about the gunfighter. Virtually every one, incidentally, depended on a Colt.

Even in their day, the histories of those gunfighters were soon encrusted with legends, so that the most conscientious research today is baffled by contradictory accounts from equally credible witnesses. For characters of such flamboyance, their life stories have a curiously similar ring. And they all seem to have known each other—at least those whose careers overlapped in time.

Take the case of the three most deadly gunslingers of the first decade after the war—Wild Bill Hickok, John Wesley Hardin, and Ben Thompson—and the thread of violence that led to an inevitable meeting between all three. That meeting, appropriately, took place in Abilene, Kansas.

During the Civil War, Texas cowhands had been off fighting the Yankees, and tens of thousands of longhorn cattle had never seen a branding iron. The open range was densely populated with ownerless beef cattle free for the taking. Roundup and branding of those mavericks was loosely called "rustling," but it was quite legal.

At the same time, the railroad pushed across the plains to Abilene, Kansas, offering transportation for those newly acquired longhorns to the eastern market. Most of the footloose cowhands of Texas wound up driving longhorn herds north to the Kansas railhead. There the hard-bitten cowhands blew off a head of steam built up during weeks of hard, dusty trail herding, posing a problem for the sedate permanent citizenry.

During 1869 and 1870, rampaging Texans in Abilene mocked the law. They shot up posters notifying them of a law against carrying firearms, tore down the jail, and when it was rebuilt, rescued at gunpoint the first prisoner, who happened to be the black cook of one of the trail herds.

In June 1870 the Abilene City Council appointed to the dangerous post of town marshal Thomas J. Smith, known as Bear River Tom because of his rough-and-tumble work as a detective for the Union Pacific Railroad during riots at Bear River, Wyoming, eighteen months before.

Bear River Tom carried two silver-plated Colts but almost never drew them. An accomplished street brawler, he beat unruly prisoners into submission and somehow escaped death—at least for the time. Incredibly, he brought some kind of order to Abilene's streets without once drawing his Colts, so far as the records show.

On November 2, 1870, he rode out with his deputy, James McDonald, to arrest Andrew McConnell for the murder of a neighbor. The law officers found their quarry and another neighbor, Moses Miles, in a prairie dugout. Bear River formally notified McConnell he was under arrest. McConnell shot him in the chest. Despite his grievous wound, Bear River grappled with McConnell and was besting him when Miles bashed Bear River on the head with a gun barrel. With a nearby ax, he cut the marshal's head half off.

Trailing no clouds of glory, Deputy McDonald rode back to Abilene and tried to explain what he was doing to keep from being bored during the fracas. Somehow, he hung on to his job, though indignation was general, for Bear River had become popular and highly respected. The pair of murderers were taken by a posse and served long penitentiary sentences.

Abilene staggered along with a succession of interim appointments. Fortunately, it was early spring, too early for the Texas invasion.

On April 15, 1871, the city council hired as town marshal James B. Hickok, widely known as Wild Bill and reputed to be the best shot, with his ivory-handled brace of Colt revolvers, on the entire frontier.

Born in northern Illinois, Hickok first came to attention on July 12, 1861, at the Overland Stage and Pony Express relay station in Rock Creek, southeastern Nebraska. Hickok was working there as a stock handler. The former owner of the station, David McCanles, accompanied by his twelve-year-old son, a cousin, and one of his farm hands, rode up to the station unarmed to collect an overdue debt from the station operator, Horace Wellman.

McCanles had a bad name as a bully and had nicknamed Hickok "Duckbill" because of a protruding upper lip Hickok later kept covered with a luxuriant mustache.

Nobody living really knows what happened next. One persuasively plausible account reports that Hickok went into the station and fired through a window, killing McCanles outright and wounding the cousin and the farm hand. Wellman dispatched the wounded cousin with a hoe, according to this account, and Hickok pursued the farm hand into the woods, where Hickok finished him off.

Four years later, in Springfield, Missouri, Hickok gave his

version of the affair to Colonel George Ward Nichols, a correspondent for *Harper's* magazine. In his account, ten members
of the "M'Kandles Gang" attacked the stage station and
Hickok singlehandedly killed them all. Later writers embroi-
dered the story with Hickok suffering a fractured skull and hid-
eous gashes, one of which had almost removed his scalp. They
found a real or imaginary Dr. Joshua Thorne, who first treated
several knife wounds, but as the years passed increased his battlefield surgery to removal of eleven bullets, all without anes-
thetic, of course.

Careful research has exploded the preposterous legend of a
"M'Kandles Gang" raid. The historical fact seems to be that
Hickok, sensing trouble coming from the powerful McCanles,
solved his problem by killing him—and with least possible
exposure of his own person to any danger. He pursued that tactic to his own violent end, and a very good tactic it was in
bloody Abilene, where the streets crawled with vicious gunmen,
none of them one whit more chivalrous than Hickok in gunning
down an enemy caught in a defenseless posture.

At the outbreak of the Civil War, Hickok acted as a civilian
scout for the Union Army in Missouri. He survived the hideously bloody battle of Wilson Creek, in August 1861. Legends abound about his Civil War escapades, but there are few
documented facts. During the winter of 1864–65, records show
that he fulfilled a hazardous assignment as a spy on Confederate
forces around Crowley's Ridge, Arkansas. He was discharged
on June 9, 1865, and he drifted up to Springfield, Missouri.

Smarting from years of cruel harassment at the hands of
Quantrill and Bloody Bill Anderson (the one-man arsenal of
Colt Navy revolvers), Union sympathizers around Springfield
improved their leisure evenings during the rest of 1865 by
tracking down former Confederate guerillas and hanging them

from the handiest tree. The atmosphere was ideal for a gunfighter.

Within weeks of his discharge, Hickok and an Arkansas gambler named Davis Tutt quarreled over a card game. On July 21, 1865, Hickok took on Tutt in a classic shootout worthy of television revival. With most of the town watching, the pair took up positions in the town square. Tutt fired first but missed; Hickok's two shots, fired so quickly they sounded like one, killed Tutt instantly at the prodigious range of seventy-five yards. Hickok was acquitted on grounds of self-defense.

Hickok became a deputy U.S. marshal at Fort Riley, Kansas, and later an army scout with Buffalo Bill Cody and Colonel George Armstrong Custer.

During his scouting days, Hickok was interviewed by Henry Morton Stanley, then a correspondent for the *Weekly Missouri Democrat* but later the author of the magnificently pompous line "Dr. Livingstone, I presume?"

Hickok improved even on the great massacre of the "M'Kandles Gang" at Rock Springs. In his latest addition to the legend, he told the breathless Stanley he had once captured fifteen killers in a Fort Leavenworth hotel. Not only that, their leader was the very first man he ever killed—white man, that is—and a search of the hotel basement unearthed eleven bodies of the gang's victims.

Perhaps Hickok's romances impressed those supposedly worldly reporters because of his imposing appearance. Stanley described him at the age of thirty-eight:

> He stands six feet one inch in his moccasins and is as handsome a specimen of a man as could be found . . . straight, broad compact shoulders, herculean chest, narrow waist, and well formed muscular limbs. A fine handsome

face, free from any blemish, a light moustache, a thin pointed nose, bluish-gray eyes, with a calm, quiet almost benignant look, yet seemingly possessing some mysterious latent power, a magnificent forehead, hair parted from the center of his forehead and hanging down behind the ears in long silky curls. He is brave, there can be no doubt.

Another legend recounts that in the winter of 1869, while running army dispatches across the Plains, Hickok was chased by a Cheyenne war party and stabbed in the thigh with a broadheaded war lance. He went to Chicago to recover. With a boyhood friend, he visited a pool parlor, where his fringed buckskin clothes and moccasins stirred a great deal of mirth.

"Everybody in your part of the country wears rawhide and picks his teeth with a bowie knife?" asked a local wag.

"No, but everyone where I come from knows who his father is."

The Chicagoans were not amused, and a general brawl with pool cues followed. Hickok and his friend left under their own power; most of his tormenters were carried home.

Despite the ridiculous legends of derring-do he encouraged or even invented, there is no doubt Hickok was a superb athlete and crack shot. Mrs. Custer, the glamorous Indian fighter's beautiful wife, added to Stanley's portrait of the army scout:

Physically he was a delight to look upon, Tall, lithe and free in every motion he made, and walked as if every muscle was perfection, and the careless swing of his body as he moved seemed perfectly in keeping with the man, the country, the time in which he lived. I do not recall anything finer in the way of physical perfection than Wild Bill when he swung himself lightly from his saddle, and with graceful, swaying steps, squarely set shoulders and well pointed head, approached our tent for orders.

One of Hickok's final army duties was to escort Senator Henry S. Wilson and a party of politicians about the frontier. In gratitude, the senator gave Hickok a fateful gift: a pair of ivory-handled New Model Army Colts that Hickok wore for the rest of his life, butts turned forward for the backhand draw that his athlete's reflexes made the fastest in the West.

Robert Kane, editor of *Outdoor World,* witnessed an exhibition of Wild Bill's skill with his Colts:

> Standing on the railroad track, in a deep cut, his pistols crackling with the regularity of an old house clock, he struck and dislodged the bleaching pebbles stuck in the face of the bank at a distance of fifteen yards.
>
> Standing about thirty feet from the shooter, one of our party tossed a quart can in the air to the height of about thirty feet. This was perforated three times before it reached the ground, twice with the right hand and once with his left.
>
> Standing between the fences of a country road, which is four rods wide, Mr. Hickok's instinct of location was so accurate that he placed a bullet in each of the fence posts on opposite sides. Both shots were fired simultaneously.

It may have been this flashy trick in his shooter's repertory that gave rise to the legend that Hickok had once killed two men simultaneously, firing one Colt forward and the other over his left shoulder to kill a brace of enemies who had tried to take him fore and aft.

Kane recounts a half dozen more trick shots and closes with the classic tin-can trick:

His last feat was to me the most remarkable of all. A quart can was thrown by Mr. Hickok himself, which dropped about ten or twenty yards distant. Quickly whipping out his weapons he fired alternately from left to right. Advancing a step with each shot, his bullets striking the earth under the can, kept it in continuous motion until his pistols were empty.

It is interesting that in the can-in-the-air shots and in the can-along-the-ground shots, Hickok alternated right and left hands with apparently near-equal skill. Many historians have argued that he was purely right-handed and carried a second Colt only as a reserve.

Kane credited Hickok's impressive skill to that same physical grace and co-ordination all witnesses reported:

No matter how elusive the target, even when shooting at objects tossed in the air, he never seemed hurried. This trait was of course natural and in part due to his superb physique, which combined and supplemented by his methods and practice and free wild life in the open, developed in him that perfect coordination of hand and eye which was essential to the perfect mastery of the one-hand gun.

Hickok put in a hitch as sheriff of Ellis County, where he patrolled the streets of Hays City with a shotgun in hand, a bowie knife sticking out of his boot top, and the two Colt .44s swinging from his belt.

One daring fellow called Sullivan got the drop on the sheriff by jumping out of an alley, his pistol already drawn. Chortling with triumph, he called on bystanders to witness the death of the famous gunfighter. While Sullivan's attention was divided, Hickok made a lightning draw and killed him.

"He talked his life away," Hickok said with contempt, for it was an error he would never be accused of. Once Hickok had the drop, he had no mercy.

After he killed another man, admittedly an unpopular bully, the citizens worried that he was trigger-happy and voted him out of office. Before leaving town, in a saloon brawl, he killed one trooper of the Seventh Cavalry Regiment and wounded another. Troopers of the Seventh were notoriously clannish and numbered many hard cases in their ranks; Hickok concluded he could not take on the U. S. Army, so he left town.

It was then that Abilene called him to be town marshal, replacing the foolhardy Bear River Tom. Hickok set up headquarters at the poker table in the Alamo Saloon and patrolled the streets as he had in Hays, armed with shotgun, bowie knife, and ivory-handled Colts.

Most of the trouble in turbulent Abilene came from the Texas cowboys who had just spent weeks on the trail and were ready for a romp in the stews of town, or from the gamblers and thieves who had flocked there to prey on the cowboys. And those Texas cowboys took some containing, for scattered among them were some of the most dangerous gunmen in the West.

Among that postwar generation of Texas gunslingers were John Wesley Hardin, who probably ran up the highest score of killings in western history, and Ben Thompson, credited by such experts as Bat Masterson, marshal of Dodge City, Kansas, and no mean gunman himself, with being the fastest and most accurate killer of the day.

John Wesley Hardin, born in 1853 to a circuit-riding Methodist preacher in Bonham, Texas, before his death, in 1895, may well have killed one man for each of his forty-two years.

He was reared in a home presided over by a cultured and gentle mother and a well-educated father, so he had excellent schooling; his collected letters show a background far superior to that of the rough cowhands with whom he associated.

Hardin reached early adolescence, a hard enough transition for any man, during the Reconstruction period, when white Texans were seething with rage over what they considered an outrageously corrupt and unjust government.

Already inflamed by the freeing of the slaves, anti-black feeling intensified as Negro troops of the victorious Union Army patrolled the state. Hardin acquired his full share of that smoldering anger.

At a cane-cutting festival, what started out as a friendly wrestling match with a newly freed black hand called Mage turned into a savage fist fight. Adult spectators broke up the fight and ran off the black.

Next morning, Hardin reported to his uncle that Mage had attacked him with a club and he had been forced to shoot. They found the young black lying in the road, clearly dying, so Hardin's elders urged him to flee to a friend's isolated ranch, there to hide from the federal army's wrath.

Some weeks later, his brother Joseph warned Hardin that a federal patrol was approaching to arrest him. He lay in wait at a creek crossing and bushwhacked the soldiers, killing two whites and one black. (A word of warning: The historian is too often forced to take the gunslinger's word for his escapades, with only rare corroboration by reliable witnesses. Most of Hardin's accepted record comes from an autobiography he wrote in prison, large sections of which could well be heavily colored by faulty memory or self-serving distortion.)

"Parties in the neighborhood took the soldiers' horses and as we burned all their effects everything was kept quiet," Hardin reported in his memoirs. The modern reader can wonder at an army so casual it would send a patrol to arrest a killer and never inquire into their fate when they did not return.

At any rate, Hardin was able to write, "Thus by the fall of 1868, I had killed four men." He was fifteen.

It is a measure of the times that shortly afterward the youngster, a wanted murderer, was hired by the school board at Pisga, in Navarro County, to teach elementary grades. He lasted only three months at that tame occupation. Though the school board offered to extend his term, he drifted back to the open road.

Already a crack shot, Hardin put in his days polishing his skill with a Colt .44, his nights packing his revolvers (like most gunmen in the cap-and-ball days, he was a two-gun man) to frontier dance halls and poker games. Still in his teens, he had acquired such a fearsome reputation that he was credited with any killing the police could not solve. Though he was nowhere near the scene, for instance, he was accused of being an accomplice of his friend Frank Polk in a killing at Corsicana, Texas. The charge made him only slightly more wanted by police than before, and he continued to stay just ahead of pursuit.

Hardin had kinfolk scattered all over Texas who were even more hospitable to the fugitive than was the general public, most of whom would harbor anybody fleeing the Yankee occupiers. Among his many cousins was Simp Dixon, a pathological killer who had sworn a mighty oath to kill Yankees as long as he lived. Any old Yankees would do.

Trapped with his dotty cousin by Union troops at Richland Bottoms, Hardin escaped only by shooting his way out, with the death of two more soldiers. Perceiving that Simp's insane vendetta boded little good for his own skin, Hardin shied away from the one-man purification crusade and hid out on the Barnett Hardin ranch.

Election of a civil government with Edmund J. Davis as governor did little to relieve pressure on the sixteen-year-old fugitive, for Hardin had the reputation of being the most deadly killer in Texas, and the newly formed Texas State Police (quite separate from the Texas Rangers) put his killing or capture among its top priorities.

Texans liked the Reconstruction state police even less than the Yankee troops, if possible, and so they spirited the young desperado out of sight whenever a police patrol appeared.

Hardin's wanderings during that winter of 1869 left a trail of bodies. In Towash, a rowdy frontier town ruled by a brutal desperado named Jim Bradley, an unarmed Hardin cleaned out a poker game, was told by Bradley he could not pocket his winnings, and was humiliated by being stripped of his boots. Bradley should have killed Hardin while he and his henchmen had the drop, for the barefoot youngster borrowed a gun even before he borrowed footwear, killed Bradley, and ran off the rest of the gang.

That winter, he killed a circus performer who, when Hardin jostled him, unwisely took offense and tried to draw a pistol. A confidence man who had tricked Hardin out of fifty dollars in gold did not survive to enjoy his triumph. As Hardin tells the story, at the payoff he deliberately let a few coins drop to the floor. "He stooped to pick them up and as he was straightening up I pulled my pistol and fired. The ball struck him between the eyes and he fell over. . . ."

During that same winter, he met Ben Thompson, J. King Fisher, and Phil Coe, all gunslingers almost as notorious as Hardin. In Evergreen, Texas, he won three hundred dollars from Bill Longley, who had started his career as a killer much

like Hardin, with the shooting of a black freedman he thought
was too uppity. Before he was hanged, in 1877, Longley killed
thirty-two men, a score rivaling Hardin's. Nevertheless, unlike
the rash Bradley, Longley meekly surrendered his losings to
Hardin, a move that probably prolonged his life by six years.

Hardin dabbled briefly in the study of law, a subject that fas-
cinated him to the end. Police pursuit forced him to break off
his formal schooling and hit the road again. According to his
memoirs, even while on the run he continued his reading
around campfires, doubled back by the law school, passed an
examination, and picked up a diploma.

Trying to get across the Louisiana border, where he would be
safe from Texas police, Hardin was mistakenly identified as another wanted killer and jailed in Marshall to await transfer to
Waco.

A fellow prisoner, who somehow had access to a Colt .45,
sold Hardin the pistol and a baggy overcoat. When Hardin rode
off toward Waco, guarded by State Police Captain Stokes and a
Jim Smolly, under the overcoat he carried slung from his shoulder on a piece of twine the Colt .45 with four loaded chambers.

Left alone briefly with Smolly at a campsite on the Trinity
River, Hardin pretended to burst into tears of vexation at the
loud-mouthed guard's insulting banter. He let his head rest
against his pony's flank. Covered by the pony, he slipped a
hand under the overcoat, cocked the Colt and dropped the
guard dead.

Trying to escape to Mexico, Hardin was caught again, this
time by a three-man state-police patrol. That night, the police
celebrated too well, sank into a drunken slumber, and never
awakened, for Hardin killed them with their own pistols.

Hardin fled to a cousin's ranch and went into the "rustling"
business. He joined a trail herd for some unaccustomed honest

labor and headed for Abilene. Along the way, he ran into a job more suited to his talents, a brawl with a band of Mexican *vaqueros*. Hardin racked up five more killings. Leaving the bodies on the prairie, he pressed on toward a possible collision with Hickok, a battle that would match two gunslingers who were already legends on the frontier.

Already in Abilene and established in his own saloon was another notorious killer, with the commonplace name of Ben Thompson. Like Hardin, Thompson had more than the usual smattering of education on the Texas frontier. He had taken honors in an Austin private school and had worked as a printer in Austin and New Orleans.

Thompson got into a brawl with a New Orleans Creole to protect a maiden's presumably unsullied honor and threw him off a horsecar. The Creole challenged him to a duel. The favored weapon of Creole society was a vicious rapier with triangular blade, an arm virtually unknown to the Texan. As the challenged, he had choice of weapons, and he naturally shied away from swordplay. Instead he proposed a barbarous scheme: that each be issued a frontiersman's bowie knife and the pair be locked blindfolded in a darkened room. The outraged Creole had no choice, for he had issued the challenge. He did not survive the bizarre encounter. Thompson fled the law back to Texas.

Composing-room chores bored the young apprentice and he took up full-time gambling, for he had discovered an uncommon talent for manipulating cards. In fact, his second killing was brought on when a gambler with some small fame as a gunfighter called him a cheat and pulled a gun. Thompson was faster.

Austin was still so wild that a Comanche war party dared to dash into the town and abduct five young girls. As one of the pursuing posse, Thompson picked off Indians till only one escaped. All the captives were rescued.

Records show that when the Civil War broke out, Ben joined the Second Cavalry Regiment in San Antonio. He proved an unruly recruit, for early in his career he killed his lieutenant and sergeant. He escaped jail and joined another cavalry outfit, which was decimated in the catastrophic battle of Lafourche Crossing, in Louisiana. After a short leave in Austin, where he married, he became a lieutenant in Colonel John Rip Ford's regiment on the Rio Grande. Colonel Ford was that old-time Ranger who had first reported to the outside world the Plains Indian's painful introduction to the Colt five-shooter at the hands of Captain Jack Hays in 1844. Rip's scratched-together regiment of boys, old men, and misfits like the murderer he accepted as a lieutenant managed to control the upper Rio Grande, confining Union forces to the mouth of the river. Indeed, it was the regiment that fought the last land battle of the war, two weeks after Lee surrendered.

Off duty in Laredo, Thompson killed two Mexicans in a gambling hall and fled to Austin. There he was jailed with his brother Billy for killing still another man, one John Coombs, again over a card game. He escaped and joined the Army for the third time. After the surrender at Appomattox, he was jailed again for the Coombs shooting, escaped, and like many other Confederate officers, crossed the border to accept a commission offered by the doomed Austrian usurper Emperor Maximilian, then in the closing days of his struggle to protect his throne from the peasant army of the Indian lawyer Benito Juárez.

While escorting an imperial-army payroll train, Thompson's regiment took a terrible mauling:

Our men fought for the train, over it, under it, around

it, it was no use, the attack was too strong to resist, the fight continued until sundown; out of the fourteen hundred splendid soldiers, we had lost over eleven hundred. Out of my fifty-eight, with which number I went into the fight, I now had but seventeen, and eight of them seriously wounded, the forty-one were not wounded they were dead, and yet I had not been touched in the flesh; my clothes had many holes in them. . . . It was suicidal to fight longer . . . in darkness and silence we left our dead comrades to the mercy of the jackals and crows.

Thompson survived the debacle at Querétaro, where the Emperor's army collapsed. The Emperor and two generals died before a firing squad, but Thompson escaped to the Atlantic Coast. Brought down in Veracruz by a virulent attack of yellow fever, he fought his way back to life and returned to Austin, where he was promptly slapped into jail on the old Coombs charge. He and his brother served two years of a ten-year sentence in the Huntsville Penitentiary.

Attracted by reports of cowboy payrolls squandered at the end of the cattle trails in Abilene, Thompson went north and formed a partnership with another Austin gambler and gunfighter named Phil Coe to open the Bull's Head Saloon, a tough gambling hell that became notorious even in callous Abilene.

With Thompson running a disreputable house in defiance of a dozen or more Abilene ordinances, with Wes Hardin coming up the Chisholm Trail saddle-weary and ready for a frolic, with Hickok, patrolling his streets, already smoldering with anger at the rowdiness of Texans, the stage was set for a confrontation between the three most famous and dangerous gunfighters in the West.

The first clash came when the city council ordered Hickok to have Thompson and Coe remove the sign over their Bull's Head Saloon because of an enormously exaggerated male organ on the eponymous bull. The famed Texas gunfighter ignored the Yankee marshal's orders. Hickok marched a team of sign painters to the saloon and stood guard with his formidable armament prominently displayed while they painted a more decorous sign. Thompson stood meekly by.

In his memoirs, Hardin gives his version of his own encounter with the famed lawman:

> Before I got to Abilene I had heard much talk of Wild Bill, who was then marshal of Abilene. He had a reputation as a killer. I knew Ben Thompson and Phil Coe were there, and had met both these men in Texas. Besides these I learned that there were many other Texans there and so, although there was a reward offered for me, I concluded to stay some time there as I knew . . . the owners of my herd "squared" me with the officials.
>
> For a long time everybody expected trouble between Thompson and Wild Bill and I soon found out that they were deadly enemies. Thompson tried to prejudice me every way he could against Bill and told me how Bill, being a Yankee, always picked southern men to kill, and especially Texans.

Then follows an extraordinary conversation, proving better than the overblown reports of gullible correspondents how feared Hickok was by his peers.

Said Hardin: "I am not doing anybody's fighting except my own. . . . If Wild Bill needs killing, why don't you kill him yourself?"

Said Thompson: "I would rather get someone else to do it."

A remarkable demonstration of prudence for two man-killers reputed to fear no living creature.

Nevertheless, Hardin's memoirs (published long after Hickok's death) insist that Hardin recovered his bravado. According to his story, he was frolicking with other Texans in a saloon when Hickok ordered them to surrender their firearms while they were inside the city limits. Hardin refused. Hickok pulled his Colts and ordered Hardin to hand over his revolvers:

> I said all right and pulled them out of the scabbard, but while he was reaching for them I reversed them and whirled them over on him with the muzzles in his face, springing back at the same time. I told him to put his pistol up, which he did. I cursed him for a long-haired scoundrel that would shoot a boy with his back to him. . . .
>
> By this time a big crowd had gathered with pistols and arms. They kept urging me to kill him. Down the street a squad of policemen were coming but Wild Bill motioned them to go back and at the same time asked me not to let the mob shoot him.

Hardin claims that he threatened the crowd if any dared raise a hand to help in what was his private fight. Hickok praised Hardin as "the gamest and quickest boy I ever saw" and offered to buy him a drink. They sat and sipped together and parted with an understanding—or so says Hardin.

Anybody who believes that story has not read the documented history of Wild Bill Hickok, who 1. was too smart and fast to be taken by that phony carnival twirl trick, and 2. if he had been taken, would have been instantly killed by the cold-blooded Hardin, and 3. if he had not been killed by Hardin, sometime during the amicable loving cup he would have killed Hardin for humiliating him publicly.

Also, there is a strange internal contradiction in Hardin's story. How could Hickok reach for Hardin's pistols if he had already drawn his own pair of Colts? Besides, there never was a "squad of policemen" in Abilene, only two deputies, including the cowardly McDonald, who would have been well out of sight.

The most telling weakness of the story is that no member of that supposed mob of angry witnesses has ever come forward to support Hardin's boast, which Hardin was careful to make only long after Hickok was dead and silent. In the gossipy West of that time, the story of Wild Bill's humiliation would have flashed in a week from the Mexican to the Canadian borders and clean to the California shore.

Though Hickok did later kill Phil Coe, Thompson's partner and himself a dangerous gunfighter, the fact is that the three most dangerous gunmen in the West never tangled. In the one documented confrontation, the painting over of the bull's offending parts, Hickok faced down Ben Thompson and made his orders stick.

All three gunslingers died violently, and all three were shot treacherously from ambush or in the back of the head, so in a sense they all died undefeated. Nevertheless, in the lone encounter between the three, Hickok came off top dog, for he ran his town his way and the other two backed away from a gun fight.

Those wild and woolly days of the first decade after the Civil War were dominated by Colt's last designs, the Navy and the New Model Army, and an assortment of derringers and other pocket pistols. By 1873 the Rollin White patent on cylinders bored through for metallic cartridges had expired, however, and soon a new pistol came out of the Colt line, one generation beyond the master, marking the end of his personal influence on the history of armament.

With expiration of the White patent, all arms makers rushed to design revolvers with bored cylinders. (Curiously, many frontiersmen rejected the superior metallic cartridge and clung to their cap-and-ball weapons for decades.)

By 1872 the Colt Armory's William Mason had patented a revolver with cartridges loaded and ejected from a side gate with ejector lying beside the barrel. The Army tested the weapon and—with an enthusiasm that would have stunned Sam after his lifelong war with a hostile Ordnance Department—ordered eight thousand for the cavalry. They called it the New Model Army Pistol of 1873, but one merchant dubbed it the Peacemaker and the name stuck.

That Peacemaker, a solid-frame, single-action six-shooter made in calibers from .45 to .476, instantly became and remains the most famous revolver ever designed. If a Western-movie or television hero stands stiff-legged in the middle of a cowtown street, his hand poised over his holster, ready to do battle with the bad guys, you can bet the prop man filled the holster with a Peacemaker.

The weapon deserves its reputation. At fifty yards the bullet penetrated 3¾ inches of white pine, at one hundred yards an impressive 3½ inches. Even at the impractical pistol range of three hundred yards, the bullet penetrated 2½ inches. The Army's formula provides that penetration of one inch of pine is the equivalent of a very dangerous or lethal wound. Also, in every test of accuracy, the Peacemaker surpassed all rivals.

The Peacemaker had only one competitor on the frontier. In 1873 Winchester produced a repeating rifle chambered for .44–40 cartridges. It swept the frontier market and today is popularly known as "the gun that won the West." Like the

Peacemaker, it is the only rifle a prop man would think of putting into a Western star's hands. Colt executives had the intelligence not to fight them but to join them by chambering one line of Peacemakers for the same .44–40 cartridge, so that droves of frontiersmen, including the entire Texas Ranger force, armed themselves with a Winchester rifle in a saddle holster, Peacemakers in belt scabbards, and bandoliers loaded with cartridges that fit either weapon.

So good was the Peacemaker, in fact, that the Colt company almost immediately after its appearance stopped manufacture of the immensely popular Navy model.

With the disappearance of the Navy, the old man's influence on revolver design had shriveled to almost nothing.

His armory still hummed along, however, its belts driving ingenious machinery, its workers outproducing competitors, the very model of the kind of mass production that was rapidly making America the industrial giant of the world. (Colt's armory had burned on February 4, 1864, but was soon rebuilt.)

Sam Colt had applied his inventive genius to the making of arms and was so good at it that to this day many think "Colt" and "revolver" are synonyms.

His real genius and his best gift to the world, however, is in those clacking, humming production lines where harnessed steam and electricity allow frail men to outwork herds of wild horses and so support a standard of living and civilization not dreamed of in fantasies of unlimited wealth when the sixteen-year-old Sam whittled his first rude revolver model out of a ship's tackle block aboard the *Corvo,* only a century and a half ago.

INDEX

Abdul Mejid I (Turkish sultan), 130
Adams, John Quincy, 62
Adams, Robert, 139
Adams, Samuel, 52–54
Adams revolver, 139, 155, 156
Alamo, 18, 198
Alden, J. D., 184–85, 195, 196
Allen pepperbox revolver, 122–23
Allsens, Adam, 106
American Institute, 26, 62, 63
Ampudia, Pedro de, 88
Anderson, Bloody Bill, 204, 205, 209
Apache Indians, 196, 197
Arista, Mariano, 83, 85, 86
Arizona, 76, 109, 195, 196
Athon, Henry, 64, 65
Austria, 118, 133, 134, 145, 190

Badger, George, 50
Ball, William, 99
Baltimore *Republic*, 21
Baltimore *Sun*, 118–19
Bassett, Abner, 10
Baton Rouge *Daily Express*, 191–92
Baxter, A. T., 13
Beauregard, Pierre, 87
Belgium, 137–38, 146–47, 149, 158
Bigelow, Sergeant, 39
Billy Bowlegs, Chief, 39
Billy the Kid, 206
Blair, F. S., 20–21
Blunt, Orison, 96
Bomford, George, 35, 50
Bow and arrow warfare, 3, 75
Boyd, E. S., 184
Boyle, Junius, 69
Brackett, Albert, 103–4
Bradley, Jim, 217, 218
Bragg, Braxton, 87
Brices Cross Roads battle, 204
British Army, 1, 72, 152, 189
British Navy, 61, 143, 152, 153
Brown, Jacob, 85, 86
Brown, John, 191, 193

Brunette (bark), 67. *See also Styx*
Bull's Head Saloon, 221, 222, 224
Burr, Aaron, 76
Burr, John, 67
Busk, Hans, 189–90

Caesar, Charles, 177
Calcutta *Englishman*, 141
Caldwell, John, 4, 5
California, 76, 82, 109, 121, 131–32
Callahan, James Hughes, 169–70
Caribbean islands, 76
Carlton, James H., 194–95
Carson, Kit, 77–79, 152
Cartridges, 67, 94, 226
Cassidy, Butch, 206
Castle Garden, 27, 58–59, 60, 62
Catlin, George, 172–74
Cattle rustling, 206, 218
Charleston *Courier*, 21
Chase, Anson, 10, 11, 12–13
Chekika (Chai-ki-ka), Chief, 42–43
Cherokee Indians, 1
Chul-le-qua (Shawnee captain), 171
Civil War, 199, 203–4, 205, 206
Clare (Ireland) *Journal*, 153
Clarke, Lewis Gaylord, 65
Cochran rifle, 23–24, 36
Cody, Buffalo Bill, 210
Coe, Phil, 217, 221, 222, 224
Collier, Elisha, 9
Collier flintlock rifle, 9
Collins Axe Company, 125
Colt, Amos, 191–92
Colt, Caldwell, 187, 197, 201
Colt, Christopher, 3, 4, 5, 6, 8, 10, 11, 17, 21, 22
Colt, Elisha, 132
Colt, Elizabeth Jarvis (Mrs. Samuel Colt), 166–67, 179, 187, 201–2
Colt, Harris, 125
Colt, James, 4, 36, 66–67, 146, 157–58, 159, 175–76, 177–78, 181–82

Colt, John, 4, 52–55, 56, 62, 63–64, 65–66, 145, 148, 165
Colt, Olivia Sargent, 5
Colt, Roswell L., 31, 33, 34
Colt, Samuel, 3, 4–18, 67, 94, 102, 109, 119–20, 121, 124, 130, 134, 136, 164, 174, 176–77, 197, 200
  Armsmear, 187, 201
  and brothers. *See* Colt, James; Colt, John
  and Caroline Henshaw. *See* Henshaw, Caroline
  Corvo cruise, 8–10, 226
  daughter, 197
  death, 200–1
  and Dudley Selden, 16, 17, 20, 21, 22, 23, 25, 26, 30, 33, 35–36, 46, 52
  harbor defense. *See* Submarine mine system
  and John Ehlers, 46, 50, 51–52, 56–57, 58, 62, 92, 138
  lobbying, 121, 123, 127, 154
  marriage to Elizabeth Jarvis, 166–67
  nitrous oxide tour, 7, 10–12, 13
  patents issued to. *See* Patents
  rifle and revolver manufacture. *See* Colt armory; Patent Arms Manufacturing Company; Whitneyville Arsenal
  and Samuel Walker, 87, 89–95, 99–102, 108. *See also* Walker, Samuel
  silver mine, 195–97
  sons, 179, 187
  and U. S. Army. *See* U. S. Army
  and William S. Harney, 30–31, 32. *See also* Harney, William S.
Colt, Samuel Caldwell (Junior), 55, 64, 65, 144–45, 148, 180–81, 197, 201, 202
Colt, Sarah Ann, 4, 5
Colt, Sarah Caldwell, 3, 5
Colt armory, 105, 110, 131, 132, 135, 144, 149, 178, 186, 187, 197, 200, 225, 226
  Civil War production, 197, 198–99, 205
  employees' welfare, 166, 167
  London operation, 139, 141–42, 144, 146, 157, 177, 179
  mass production, 125–26, 138, 159–62, 226
  pay scale, 162–63

South Meadows factory, 148, 162, 165–66
  wicker furniture manufacture, 167
  workers at Sam's funeral, 200–1
Colt hallmark designs, 15, 100
Colt repeating rifle, 18, 57, 77, 174
  army testing, 23–25, 45
  navy testing, 40–41, 45–46
  on sale, 26–27
  Texas Ranger-Indian wars, 74, 75, 89
Colt revolvers, 9–10, 11, 18, 40, 78–79, 84, 85, 89, 91, 136, 137, 173, 174, 204, 206, 226
  Dragoon Number 1 (Improved Holster Model), 113–14, 115, 117, 122, 123, 124, 126, 127, 130, 132, 135, 137–38, 140, 193, 194
  five-shooter, 36, 74, 77, 200
  hallmark, 100
  Navy, 135–36, 199, 203, 204, 205, 224, 226
  New Model Army of 1873, 225
  New Model Army Pistol, 194, 198, 212, 224
  New Model Navy, 136, 149
  No. 5, 34, 36, 38, 51, 56, 96
  Patent Repeating Pistol, 97–98
  Paterson, 92, 96, 102
  Peacemaker, 93, 136, 225
  pocket pistols, 121, 122, 124, 132, 137–38
  six-shooter, 93, 128, 203, 204, 205
  Texas Paterson, 36, 38, 135
  Walker Colt, 81, 93, 102, 107, 109, 110, 111, 113, 117
Comanche Indians, 74, 75, 78, 84, 87, 89, 91, 100, 171–72, 219–20
Confederacy, 198, 199, 200
Confederate forces, 104, 182, 194, 203, 204, 209, 220
Conrad, Charles, 139, 140
Coombs, John, 220, 221
Craig, H. B., 186
Crawford, George, 124, 126
Creek Indians, 1
Crimean War, 152, 155, 163, 164, 179
Crystal Palace Exhibition, 136
Curtis, Edward, 55
Custer, George Armstrong, 210
Custer, Mrs. George Armstrong, 211–12

Dana, Charles A., 63
Davis, Edmund J., 217
Davis, Garrett, 86

Davis, Jefferson, 87, 103
Deming, Henry C., 201
Democratic Review, 54
Dennett, Charles F., 141, 144, 193
Devos-Sera, M., 138
Dickens, Charles, 47, 159–62, 178
Dickerson, Edward, 131, 137, 144, 154
Dobbin, J. D., 175
Dragoon Number 1 pistol, 113–14, 115, 117, 122, 123, 124, 126, 127, 130, 132, 135, 137–38, 140, 193, 194
Dragoons, U. S. Army, 84, 169
2d, 28, 32, 44, 117, 126

Eaton, Mr. and Mrs. Amos B., 132
Ehlers, John, 46, 50, 51, 52, 56–57, 58, 62, 92, 138
Ellsworth, Henry, 11
Emathla, Charley, 29
Emuckfaw battle, 1
England, 61, 68, 145
Crimean War, 152, 163, 164
See also British listings
Enotachopco Creek battle, 1
Europe, revolutions in, 117–18
Evening Star, 44
Ewell, Richard, 87

Farragut, David, 102
Fillmore, Millard, 134
1st Illinois Volunteers, 110
Fisher, J. King, 217
Five-shooter, 36, 74, 77, 200
Flintlock rifles, 1, 2, 9
Florida. *See* Seminole Wars
Floyd, John, 185–86, 187, 188, 193, 220
Ford, John Salmon (Rip), 170 72, 220
Forrest, Nathan Bedford, 199, 203–4
Fort Laramie *Daily Times*, 132–33
Fort Texas (Brown), 83, 84, 85, 86
Fosbery, G. V., 156
France, 117–18, 145, 190
Crimean War, 152, 163, 164
Franklin, Benjamin, 3
Franklin, John, expedition, 142–44
Fraser, A. V., 55
Frémont, John C., 77
French, S. G., 128
Frontier warfare, 170–71
Fuller, John, 36
Fulton, Robert, 2, 8, 48

Gain twist technique, 113
Garibaldi, Giuseppe, 120, 193
Gettysburg battle, 2
Gibson, Samuel, 12
Gilmer, Thomas W., 68
Governors Island garrison, 50–51
Grant, U. S., 86
Gregory, Francis, 59
Guadalupe Hidalgo Treaty, 109, 114
Gunfighters, 204, 206, 208, 209, 212, 214, 216, 219, 221
two-gun, 172, 207, 212, 216
Gunpowder experiments, 7
Gunsmiths, 2, 10, 12–13, 95, 96, 97, 99, 115, 126, 138, 175
Gwin, William, 128

Hackett, Baron, 24
Hackett rifle, 24, 36
Harbor defense system. *See* Submarine mine system
Hardin, John Wesley, 206, 214–19, 221, 222, 223, 224
Hare, Robert, 73
Harney, William S., 28, 30–31, 32, 39–40, 42–43, 43–44, 44–45, 104–5, 108, 117, 126, 129–30, 186, 188
Harpers Ferry, 191, 192, 193
Harper's magazine, 209
Hartford *Courant*, 69, 199
Hartford *Daily Times*, 164
Harwood, Andrew, 46
Hawkins, John, 17
Hays, Alexander, 154
Hays, John Coffee, 74, 75, 78, 80, 81, 84, 87, 88, 89, 91, 100, 103, 108, 117, 124, 127, 135, 152
Heinzelman, Samuel Peter, 195
Henry, Joseph, 73
Henry, P. W., 44
Henry, William R., 170
Henshaw, Caroline (alias Julia Leicester), 17–18, 54–55, 63, 64–65, 66, 144–45, 148, 179, 180, 181, 190, 201
Herrera, José Joaquin, 83, 102–3
Hickok, James B. (Wild Bill), 206, 208–14, 221, 222, 223, 224
Hockley, George W., 36
Hood, John B., 182
Horsehead design, 15
Horseshoe Bend battle, 1
Household Words, 159–62
Houston, Sam, 36, 79–80, 81, 82, 120, 121, 187

Howard, G. T., 127–28
Hoyt, Jesse, 34
Hungary, 118, 130, 133
Hunt, Memucan, 37

India, 144, 156
Indiana Volunteers, 103–4
Indians, 1, 3, 75
  Apache, 196, 197
  Cherokee, 1
  Comanche, 74, 75, 78, 84, 87, 89, 91, 100, 171–72, 219–20
  Confederacy, 1
  Creek, 1
  Kichai, 171
  Kiowa, 78
  Papago, 197
  Pimo, 197
  Plains, 2, 74, 75, 152, 172, 193, 220
  Seminole, 28–30, 39–40, 43–44, 169–70
  Shawnee, 171
  "Spanish," 39, 42, 105
  Tonkawa, 182
Iron Jacket (Comanche chief), 171

Jackson, Andrew, 1, 19–20
Jacobi, Moritz Hermann von, 50
Jaeger rifle, 95
James, Frank and Jesse, 205
Japan, 140–41, 174–75
Jarvis, Richard, 176, 202
Jarvis, William, 166
Jesup, General, 30–31, 83
Johnston, Albert Sidney, 86
Johnston, J. E., 194
Jones, Thomas Catesby, 56
Joslin, Milton, 176
Juárez, Benito, 220

Kane, E. K., 142–43
Kane, Robert, 212–13
Kansas, 172, 204, 205, 210, 214
  Abilene gunfighting, 206, 207–8, 214, 219, 221, 222
Kichai Indians, 171
Kingman, General, 188
Kiowa Indians, 78
Kossuth, Louis, 118, 130, 133

Lafourche Crossing battle, 220
Lamar, Mirabeau Buonaparte, 36
Landers, G. A., 119–20, 130–31, 176
Lane, Joseph, 107, 108, 109
Laughing gas. *See* Nitrous oxide
Lawrence, Samuel, 8–9

Lawton, Pliny, 22–23, 25, 31, 34, 38
Leavitt, Daniel, 24
Leavitt rifle, 24
Lee, Robert E., 86, 104, 187, 193, 220
Leicester, Julia. *See* Henshaw, Caroline
Lincoln, Abraham, 199
Literary Museum, 150
Lobbying, 115, 121, 123, 127, 154
London *Times,* 168
Longley, Bill, 217–18
Longstreet, James, 87
Louisville *Journal,* 37

McCanles, David, 208, 209
McClellan, George, 104
McConnell, Andrew, 207
McCulloch, Ben, 81, 103, 124, 129, 135, 198
McDonald, James, 207, 208, 224
"M'Kandles Gang," 209, 210
McLaughlan, Captain, 57
McNeill, William Gibbs, 56
Macondray, F. W., 132
Manby, Charles, 138, 139, 142
Mann, A. Dudley, 133
Marcy, W. L., 105, 114, 117, 120–21, 124, 125
Marshall, James, 122
Mason, John, 111, 112, 113
Mason, William, 225
Massachusetts Arms Company, 133, 137, 138
Mass production, 125–26, 138, 226
  Dickens' description, 159–62
Masterson, Bat, 214
Meade, George G., 86
Mexican Army, 81, 84, 85, 86
Mexican War, 85–88, 102–9, 114, 120, 121, 134
Mexico, 76, 79, 82, 83, 109, 124, 169–70, 220–21
Miles, Moses, 207
Miller, William Henry, 115, 116, 133
Mississippi Rifles, 87, 103
Missouri, 204, 205, 209–10
Mobile Bay battle, 102
Monterrey battle, 86–88
Moore, W. W., 37, 40
Morgan, George W., 129
Morgan, John Hunt, 203
Mormons, 123–24, 142
Morse, Samuel F. B., 20, 66, 73
Mounted Infantry, U. S. Army, 117
Mounted Rifles, U. S. Army, 88, 169

Navy Model revolvers, 135–36, 199, 203, 204, 205, 224, 226
New Mexico, 76, 78, 82, 109
New Model Army pistol, 194, 198, 212, 224, 225
New Orleans battle, 1
Newton, William E., 137–38
New York *Courier and Enquirer*, 25, 26
New York *Emporium*, 98, 99
New York *Enquirer*, 40
New York *Evening Post*, 59
New York *Herald*, 60, 192–93
New York *Journal of Commerce*, 178
New York *Morning Express*, 98, 99, 102
New York *Sun*, 54, 60, 74
New York *Times*, 182, 199
New York University, 66
New York *Weekly Herald*, 42
Nichols, George Ward, 209
Niles National Register, 61, 63
Nitrous oxide, 7, 10–12, 13
No. 5 pistol, 34, 36, 38, 51, 56, 96
Nolan, Philip, 77
North Carolina (gunboat), 59, 60, 63
Nueces Strip, 83, 86
Nutting, Mighill, 38

Ogden, Elias, 52
Olmstead, Frederick Law, 132
Oppen, Friedrich August Kunow Waldemar von, 179–81, 190
Ormsby, O. L., 100
Osceola (Seminole warrior), 29, 30
Outdoor World, 212
Overland Stage and Pony Express, 208

Papago Indians, 197
Paredes, Mariano, 83, 103
Patent Arms Manufacturing Company, 21, 22–23, 26, 31–33, 34, 35–36, 37, 38, 46, 47, 50–51, 52, 56–57, 58, 62, 92, 99
Patents, 11, 40, 99, 137–38
    England, 17
    foreign renewals, 130
    France, 18
    infringement suit, 133–37
    Scotland, 17
    United States, 11, 18, 19, 130, 153–54, 183–88
Paterson company. *See* Patent Arms Manufacturing Company
Paterson revolver, 92, 96, 102

Patten, Joseph H., 74
Payne, John Howard, 63, 65
Peacemaker (cannon), 68
Peacemaker (revolver), 93, 136, 225
Peacemaker (title), 102
Pearson, John, 13–17 *passim*, 21–22, 23
Percussion cap, 3, 20
Perpigna, M., 18
Perrine, Henry, 42
Perry, Matthew C., 140–41, 174–75
Pierce, Franklin, 105
Pike, Zebulon, 77
Pimo Indians, 197
Pistols. *See* Revolvers (pistols)
Plains Indians, 2, 74, 75, 152, 172, 193, 220
Polk, Frank, 216
Polk, James K., 82, 86, 88, 94, 115, 116, 122
Pony-express riders, 172
Porter, Solomon, 148

Quantrill's Raiders, 204, 205, 209

Real, Joaquín, 106
Reconstruction era, 205–6, 215, 217
Revolvers (pistols)
    Adams, 139, 155, 156
    Allen pepperbox, 122–23
    Colt. *See* Colt revolvers
Rifles
    Army competition, 23–25
    breech-loading, 24, 36
    chambered cylinder, 10, 11
    Cochran, 23–24, 36
    Collier flintlock, 9
    Colt. *See* Colt repeating rifle
    flintlock, 1, 2, 9
    Hackett, 24, 36
    Jaeger, 95
    Leavitt, 24
    magazine-loading, 23–24, 36
    reloading, 3
    Winchester repeating, 225–26
Rio Grande, 81, 83, 109, 220
Root, Elisha, 8, 125, 131, 167, 179, 193, 194
Rosas, Juan Manuel de, 140
Roughing It (Twain), 123
Rusk, Thomas J., 112, 114, 115, 116, 117, 120–21, 124–25, 139–40
Russia, 145, 153, 155, 176–77, 190
    Crimean War, 152, 155, 163, 164
    Leshgian chief/Colt revolver story, 150–52, 160

Sabin, Edwin, 78
Sandy Hook gunnery station, 45
Santa Anna, Antonio López de, 18, 81, 102–3, 104, 105–6, 109
Santa Fe raid, 79, 83
Sargeant, Luther P., 115, 163–64
Scott, Winfield, 102, 103, 105–6, 109
Second Cavalry (Confederacy), 220
2d Cavalry, U. S. Army, 182
2d Dragoons, U. S. Army, 28, 32, 44, 117, 126
2d Infantry Regiment, U. S. Army, 195
Selden, Dudley, 16, 17, 20, 21, 22, 23, 25, 26, 30, 33, 35–36, 46, 52
Selden, Joseph, 17
Seminole Indians, 28–30, 39–40, 43–44
  in Mexico, 169–70
Seminole Wars, 28–30, 39–40, 61, 79, 83, 89, 120, 129, 186
Seventh Cavalry, U. S. Army, 214
Seyd Seyd Bin Sultan Bin Ahmed, 42
Seymour, Thomas, 134, 201
Shaw, Joshua, 3
Shawnee Indians, 171
Sherman, William T., 86, 132, 182
Sigma (reporter), 69, 72
Six-shooter, 93, 128, 203, 204, 205
Slamb, Levi D., 88
Slate & Brown, 99
Slave empire dream, 76–77, 79, 82, 171
Slaves, 4, 169, 170
Slidell, John, 82, 83
Smith, Persifer, 132
Smith, Thomas J. (Bear River Tom), 207–8, 214
Smith, William T., 7
Smith & Wesson, 156–57
Smolly, Jim, 218
Somerville, Alexander, 80
Sonora Exploring and Mining Company, 195–97
Southard, Samuel, 49, 50
Southill, J., 145, 147–48
"Spanish" Indians, 39, 42, 105
Spencer, John C., 63
Stanley, Henry Morton, 210–11
Steam engine, 162, 178
Stevens, Joshua, 115, 116, 133
Stewart, James A., 185
Stokes, Captain, 218
Stoudenmire, Dallas, 206
Stuart, J. E. B., 193
Sturgis, S. D., 203–4

Styx (bark), 69–73
Submarine mine system, 7–8, 47–50, 51–52, 67, 79, 165
  demonstrations, 58–60, 61, 68–73
  moving-vessel target, 59–62, 72
  stock corporation, 51, 55–56
  underwater-battery secret, 56, 61–62, 73
Sutter, John Augustus, 122
Sutton, Captain, 127–28

Tacubaya, Armistice of, 106
Talcott, George, 94–95, 101, 116, 120 121, 124, 125, 131, 133, 139–40, 149, 176, 186
Tallahassee *Floridian*, 42–43
Taylor, Zachary, 30, 83–84, 85, 86, 87, 88, 103, 109, 111, 133, 134
Telegraph, 66, 73, 79, 165
Tennessee militiamen, 1, 3
Texas, 3, 109, 205, 206, 215, 217
  annexation, 68, 82, 83, 134
  cattle drives, 207, 208, 214
  secession, 198
Texas, Republic of, 36, 37, 40, 68, 74–75, 79, 146
Texas Paterson pistol, 36, 38, 135
Texas Rangers, 74, 75, 77–78, 80–81, 82, 84, 85, 86, 87–88, 89, 91, 103–4, 106, 109, 127, 128–29, 168–74, 187, 226
Texas Regiment, 127–28
Texas Panhandle, 170
Texas State Police, 217
Thompson, Ben, 206, 214, 217, 219–21, 222, 224
Thompson, Billy, 220
Thorne, Joshua, 209
Thornton, W. A., 85
Tinfoil-wrapped cartridges, 67, 94
Tobin, G. H., 128–29
Tonkawa Indians, 182
Torrey, David K., 124, 170
Tracy, Harry, 206
Triangle Trade, 4
True & Davis, 12
Tutt, Davis, 210
Twain, Mark, 123
Two-gun men, 172, 207, 212, 216
Tyler, John, 47, 50, 68, 82
Tyler, Mrs. John, 82

Union forces, 104, 193, 198, 203–4, 205, 209, 215, 220
Union Pacific Railroad, 207
University of Pennsylvania, 73

Upshur, Abel P., 50, 56, 59, 60, 62, 68
U. S. Army, 20, 106, 130, 188
  cavalry, 182, 193, 225
  Colt's efforts to sell arms to, 19–20, 23–25, 31, 34–35, 45, 47, 79, 88–89, 112, 113, 114
  Colt's sales to, 31–33, 50–51, 94–95, 225
  commercial moonlighting, 132
  Dragoons, 84, 169
  1st Cavalry Regiment, 193
  Mounted Infantry Regiment, 117
  Mounted Rifles Regiment, 88, 169
  New Model Army pistol, 194, 198, 212, 224, 225
  Ordnance Department, 23, 24, 35, 79, 94–95, 101, 110, 112, 116, 120, 128–29, 131, 133, 186
  Pacific Department, 132
  rifle testing, 45
  2d Cavalry Regiment, 182
  2d Dragoons, 28, 32, 44, 117, 126
  2d Infantry Regiment, 195
  Seminole Wars, 28–30, 39–40, 79
  Seventh Cavalry Regiment, 214
  West Point Rifle competition, 23–25, 30
U. S. Marines, 41, 57
U. S. Navy
  Colt's harbor defense system, 47–50, 51–52, 55, 58, 59, 60, 62
  Navy Colts, 135–36, 149, 199, 203, 204, 205, 224, 226
  Pacific Squadron, 56
  reports on Colt repeating rifle, 40–41, 45–46

Van Buren, Martin, 42
Veracruz siege, 102, 103

Walker, Isaac P., 125, 127
Walker, Jonathan, 107
Walker, Joseph E., 13, 14
Walker, Samuel H., 81, 84, 85, 87, 88, 107–9
  and Colt, 87, 89–95, 99–102, 108
  Colt hallmark design, 100
Walker Colt, 81, 93, 102, 107, 109, 110, 111, 113, 117
Wallace, Big Foot, 81
Walsh, Michael, 154
Ware, Massachusetts, 5, 6
  nitrous oxide experiments, 7, 10
  submarine explosion, 7–8, 125
Warrington, Lewis, 58
Washington *Daily National Intelligencer*, 69
Washington *Globe*, 21, 41
Washington *Post*, 20–21
Webster, Daniel, 50, 134
Weekly Missouri Democrat, 210
Wellman, Horace, 208
Wesson, Daniel, Edwin, and Frank, 115–16, 131, 133
White, Rollin, 156–57, 224, 225
Whitney, Eli, Jr., 95–96, 98, 99
Whitneyville Arsenal, 95, 98, 105
Wiggins, Oliver, 78
Wild Cat (Seminole chief), 169, 170
Wilkinson, James, 76, 77
Williamson, Three Leg, 174
Wilson, Henry S., 212
Winchester repeating rifle, 225–26
Worth, William, 87
Wynkoop, F. H., 108

Young, Brigham, 123
Younger, Cole, 205

Zabriski, C. B., 36, 51, 110–11, 115